Community and Conflict in Eastwood

A Study From the Nottinghamshire Coalfield Before 1914

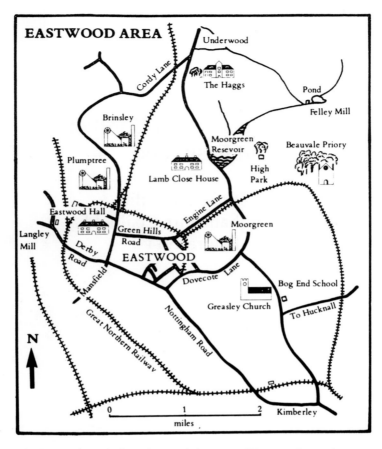

EASTWOOD AREA

Underwood

Cordy Lane

The Haggs

Pond

Felley Mill

Brinsley

Moorgreen
Resevoir

Beauvale Priory

Plumptree

Lamb Close House

High
Park

Eastwood Hall

Engine Lane

Moorgreen

Langley
Mill

Green Hills
Road

Derby
Road

EASTWOOD

Mansfield

Dovecote Lane

Bog End School

Greasley Church

To Hucknall

N

Great Northern Railway

Nottingham Road

0   1   2

miles

Kimberley

The Eastwood area in the early twentieth century. The map shows the main features of the early twentieth century industrial infrastructure including three of the Barber Walker pits: Brinsley, High Park and Moorgreen.

Community and Conflict in Eastwood

A Study From the
Nottinghamshire Coalfield
Before 1914

Roger Moore

DEPARTMENT OF ADULT EDUCATION
UNIVERSITY OF NOTTINGHAM

Centre for Local History Occasional Papers No. 7

First published in 1995 by
The Department of Adult Education
Education Building
University Park
Nottingham NG7 2RD

© Roger Moore, 1995

ISBN 1 85041 080 1

Printed in England by Technical Print Services, Nottingham

Contents

List of Illustrations

Acknowledgements

The author would like to express grateful thanks to the following for permission to reproduce the illustrations listed:

Mr George Hardy for the map of Eastwood and the photograph of T.P. Barber. Both appeared originally in George Hardy and Nathaniel Harris, *A D.H. Lawrence Handbook* (Moorland Publishing, 1983).

University of Nottingham for the photographs of W.E. Hopkin and Moorgreen Colliery; the originals are held in the Lawrence Collection, University Library.

Nottinghamshire County Council for the cover photograph, Working Underground, High Park Colliery and Eastwood Miner at Leisure.

The cover photograph and illustrations 5 and 6 are part of the Cobb Collection. All were taken circa 1910 by the Rev. F.W. Cobb, rector of Eastwood 1907-17. The collection is now held in the Nottinghamshire Local Studies Library, Angel Row, Nottingham. The author is indebted to Dorothy Ritchie for her help in the selection.

I

Introduction

As the twentieth century draws to a close it becomes ever more apparent that the British coal-mining industry is in a state of near terminal decline. This decline has been discernible both in terms of output and numbers employed for much of the century. Peak output was reached in 1913 when a figure of 292 million tons was registered by a workforce of something in excess of one million. Thereafter both fell steadily apart from a slight recovery in the 1930s. By the 1960s, production had dipped below 200 million tons and by the beginning of the present decade did not reach even 100 million. Despite the outcry over the government's plans in the Autumn of 1992, the White paper, published 25 March 1993, envisaged almost a total obliteration with a mere 12 pits and a workforce of about 30,000, whose future could scarcely be guaranteed in an energy market described as 'competitive'.

This process of decline has been accompanied by turmoil as miners, their communities and mining unions have attempted to come to grips with the attendant problems. The most obvious result has been conflict, often major conflicts, between employers and labour right from the great lock-out of 1893 until the equally herculean struggle of 1984-5. The unions in particular have experienced a time of prolonged trauma during the relatively short period since 1970. From having power which led one former Conservative premier to comment, perhaps apocryphally, that no one in their right mind would risk an engagement with the NUM, the mining unions have undergone a reversal succinctly summed up by the treasurer of the Durham Miners' Gala. Commenting on the likely demise of that quintessential event in the labour as well as the mining calendar, he remarked 'you can see what's happened, we've been decimated'.[1]

In these circumstances there is inevitably a review and debate about the place of the coal industry and its workforce in the late twentieth century economy and about the social implications of the changes experienced. Equally it is not unreasonable to argue that some re-examination of the long-term historical trends is required for it is worth considering whether the present situation is, to some degree at least, a resolution of trends operational over the period of the last century. Looked at from this perspective, the Nottingham-shire coalfield is an especially interesting case, not least because it has been the subject of two such studies recently, one looking at the situation between the wars[2] and the second attempting to unravel more recent events.[3] This present study aims to look at the picture before 1914 and, in a rather more restricted manner, examine the situation in one individual community: Eastwood. The justification for this is twofold. In the first place it will be possible to look at the mainsprings of the community in some depth considering in particular the reactions and inter-reactions of both workforce and employ-ers in a complex and difficult situation. Secondly, and perhaps of even more obvious significance, this community is of special interest because it is, in the view of the major authority on East Midlands coal mining, the original base of the breakaway Spencer Union which so distracted the miners in Nottinghamshire between the wars.[4]

At the outset it has to be admitted that there are serious methodological issues to be addressed in the approach adopted. In the first place it is dangerous to generalise about mining communities on the basis of one case study, especially on the crucial relationship between underlying value systems and the nuts and bolts of industrial relations. Nevertheless some broadly agreed framework is necessary if the present study is to make sense.

In reality the nineteenth century industrialist, whether operating a factory or a coal-mine, did not always square with the traditional stereotypes presented to us either by free-marketeers like Adam Smith or by Marx, Engels and their followers. There is evidence of an element of paternalism in the employers' world view and this invariably took the form of attempts to build a sense of community which, it was thought, would be a force binding masters and men together, emphasising that there were shared interests. The driving motivation was undeniably economic and practical. In the coal industry in particular, given the isolated nature of many of the mining operations, the owners were compelled to make provision for reasonable housing as a means of attracting the necessary labour. Other facilities were also deemed essential, hence the contribution to the building or endowment of churches and chapels and of leisure facilities such as libraries and reading rooms often in the forms of 'mechanics' institutes'. There was often an interest in education and even, following the representative reorganisation of local government in the late nineteenth century, an attempt to secure political leadership of the community. Inevitably with this there is a clearly developing emphasis on the notion of social control. Ideologically this could be dressed up in the rather more moralistic terms of employers having a responsibility to look after the interests of their workforce on the grounds that the workers were incapable of doing this for themselves. J.S. Mill made this point as early as 1848 when he wrote 'The rich should be in loco parentis to the poor guiding and restraining them like children. Of spontaneous action on their part there should be no need. They should be called on for nothing but to do their day's work and be moral and religious'.[5] In practical terms, however, what employers sought to create was some sort of bastard re-incarnation of the medieval village: in sociological terms a 'deference community' or, put more simply, a 'company town'.[6] In the East Midlands mining area this concept had already been developed to some extent by the Butterley Company in Derbyshire[7] and it was to be carried further, reaching its apogee in the opening up of the Dukeries coalfield in North Nottinghamshire during the period between the wars.[8] Essentially employers who espoused this view of the world saw the creation of such communities as a means of stabilising and strengthening their enterprises. They were anxious to exert control over their workforce but, at root, this was not to be achieved by superior power but by promoting the idea that the interests of master and man were identical.[9]

The initial response of the employees across the industrial scene, but especially in coal-mining to this approach was confused, and, indeed, the confusion remains to this day, as recent events in the Nottinghamshire coalfield have made abundantly plain.[10] Basically there were two responses: one, accepting, co-operating and deferential, the other, oppositional and confrontational. This division is seen quite clearly across the working-class movement in the later nineteenth century and not only affected the development of the trade unions but also had wide-ranging political repercussions. However the confusion was made especially acute in coal-mining because of the nature of the work, the organisation of the industry and the underlying value system of the miners. Thus, while it is true to say that there was a tradition of acting together, of solidarity, there was also the equally strong tradition of the 'independent collier'.[11] In the East Midlands this was further strengthened by the continuation of the sub-contracting system in which a considerable degree of control was delegated by the owners and management to the so-called 'butties'.

However, to leave the discussion there would be simplistic and misleading for the response of employees was more complex. To understand this better, it is helpful to return to the seminal analysis of E.P. Thompson, which, while rooted in the earlier part of the nineteenth century remains relevant in the consideration of the later period.[12] In contradiction to the employers' paternalistic notion of 'community', there arose the concept of 'mutuality' in which 'the self respecting artisan'[13] developed networks of social support which in turn helped promote a growing political consciousness, a well established, disciplined 'working class culture of ... independence and complexity'.[14] By these means, the working class would, and did, break 'the crust of fatalism, deference and need, within which their lives were enclosed'.[15] The institutions through which this progress was made were essentially the Friendly Society and the trade unions but direct, even confrontational political activity was to form a crucial part of the process and it is especially important to notice the emphasis that Luddism receives in Thompson's work.

In essence Thompson follows the Marxist tradition which sees a clear and unambiguous relationship between class and community and hence collective action. Among those who have followed this line with particular reference to the coal industry is the distinguished Labour historian Henry Pelling. Thus he comments '... all students of mining villages have stressed their extraordinary cohesion which must be ascribed in part to their isolation and concentration upon one type of employment, in part to the common dangers of the miner's life'.[16]

But a contrary view has recently been advanced by David Gilbert which challenges the neo-Marxist assumption that class, collective action and political radicalism are all clearly and even automatically linked.[17] What makes this so immediately apposite is that it is based in part on special studies of Nottinghamshire and within the county, another individual mining community, Hucknall. At the same time, broadening the base of the argument, he looks comparatively at the very difference situation in South Wales.

Considering the evidence provided by these two areas, Gilbert draws up three distinctive models of coal-mining communities. The first is indeed very similar to the conventional stereotype: socially homogeneous, closed, isolated, with the institutions controlled by the miners themselves. The second is similar but with the important exception that the employer or company has an imortant, influential role and the 'paternalistic authority' of the owners was much in evidence. Interestingly, the point already made above that this was an echo of past social relationships is strikingly confirmed by the discovery of '... a direct lineage between the pre-industrial authority of the squirearchy and that of the coal owners.' The third type was a more mixed community in which miners lived in close proximity to other workers and where '... a sense of separate communal identity [was] lacking.' The distinctions are to be treated with caution for it must be remembered that '... the character of any particular mining community [is] the result of a particular history' but nevertheless such models do '... provide a useful starting point for understanding the processes of historical change'.[18]

We have now a broad general framework which gives us some idea of the word 'community' and against which the events in one relatively small area may be viewed in a meaningful way. At the same time however it will also be necessary to emphasise the importance of considering Eastwood within the context of the Nottinghamshire coalfield as a whole. The experience of this one community thus makes more sense and its significance becomes much clearer. Therefore, while the core of the study consists of an analysis of the two 'communities' and the nature of the conflict between them, this has to be preceded by an examination of the main features of the wider area in the pre-1914 period with a special emphasis on the character of industrial relations.

However, before looking at the detail, it is necessary for a word of explanation on the sources used. Almost inevitably a good deal of reliance has been placed on the back files of the local newspaper *The Eastwood and Kimberley Advertiser*. The reporting of the industrial disputes which convulsed the area throughout much of the period 1907-12 is extremely detailed and, as a result, gives a clear insight into the actions and motives of both coal owners and miners. Nevertheless there still remains the question of the newspaper's even-handedness. In fact, there is evidence that the editor did try to steer a middle path, to report the facts as best he could and let his readers make up their own minds. On some occasions he did feel it necessary to come off the fence. Thus, towards the end of 1907 reporting a growing deadlock between employers and men, the paper appealed to the latter for moderation and 'compromise rather than allow matters to drift into complete deadlock'.[19] Later the pro-employer stance became even more marked, deploring the mens' strike action and commenting on the owners' 'excellent name for the consideration they have shown their employees'.[20] But such hyperbole was rare and perhaps more typical was the way in which the paper roundly criticised both sides for their intransigence in failing to seek a reasonable settlement while expressing concern at the mounting privation resulting from the strike.[21] However, perhaps even more reassuring as an indication of the paper's reliability as a historical source is the fact that, throughout this period, it allowed the young W.E. Hopkin, already a prominent progressive politician in the town, to contribute a weekly column of personal views which were often extremely radical, even socialist, in content.[22] It may perhaps be safely concluded that the editor, like so many local newspapermen of the period, saw his responsibility to all sections of the community he served. He can be said neither to be in the pocket of the coal owners nor excessively sympathetic to the cause of their employees. The evidence drawn from this source then may be regarded, in terms of reliability, with some confidence.

References

1.   Quoted in *The Guardian*, 12 July 1993.

2.   C.P. Griffin, *Nottinghamshire Miners Between the Wars: The Spencer Union Revisited* (Department of Adult Education, Nottingham University, 1984).

3.   W. J. Morgan and K. Coates, *The Nottinghamshire Coalfield and the British Miners' Strike, 1984-85* (Department of Adult Education, Nottingham University, 1989).

4.   A.R. Griffin, *The Miners of Nottinghamshire, Vol. II, 1914-1944* (Allen and Unwin, 1962), pp. 96-7. On George Spencer himself, there is a very convenient biography in J.M. Bellamy and J. Saville (eds.) *Dictionary of Labour Biography, Vol. I* (Macmillan, 1972).

5.   J.S. Mill, *Principles of Political Economy, Vol. II*, (1848). Quoted

in H. Newby, 'Paternalism and Capitalism' in R. Scase (ed.), *Industrial Society* (Allen and Unwin, 1977).

6.   There have been a number of studies of attempts to create such communities. See especially, Robert Moore, *Pitmen Preachers and Politics* (Cambridge University Press, 1974) in which chapter 3 looks at the activities of the Durham coalowners, Joseph Pease and partners. For a more general discussion of the phenomenon as it affected the factory communities of the textile districts, see P. Joyce, *Work Society and Politics: The Culture of the Factory in Late Victorian England* (Harvester Press, 1980), especially chapters 3 and 4.

7.   See R. Christian, *Butterley Brick: Two Hundred Years in the Making* (London, 1990) as an interesting account directly commissioned by the latter-day company.

8.   For the details of this see R.J. Waller, *The Dukeries Transformed: The Social and Political Development of a Twentieth Century Coalfield* (Oxford, 1983).

9.   Joyce, *Work Society and Politics*, p. 94.

10.   Morgan and Coates, *The Nottinghamshire Coalfield*.

11.   For an extended discussion of this see R. Samuel (ed.) *Miners, Quarrymen and Saltworkers* (RKP, 1977), and R. Harrison (ed.) *The Independent Collier* (Harvester Press, 1978).

12.   E.P. Thompson, *The Making of the English Working Class* (Penguin edition, 1968), especially chapter 12.

13.   *Ibid.,* p. 457.

14.   *Ibid.,* p. 658.

15.   *Ibid.,* p. 896.

16.   H. Pelling, *Popular Politics and Society in Late Victorian Britain* (Macmillan, 1969), p. 46.

17.   D. Gilbert, *Class Community and Collective Action: Social Change in Two British Coalfields 1850-1926* (Oxford, 1992).

18. *Ibid.*, pp. 44-47. The whole theoretical issue of the nature of mining communities and their predilliction or otherwise to collective action is discussed at considerable length in chapter 2, pp. 9-53.

19. *Eastwood and Kimberley Advertiser*, 20 December 1907.

20. *Advertiser*, 3 January 1908.

21. *Advertiser*, 14 February 1908.

22. For a detailed analysis of Hopkin's beliefs see below, Section IV.

II

The Nottinghamshire Coalfield Before 1914

While coal has been mined in appreciable quantities in Nottinghamshire since the late sixteenth century, the major expansion and development of the field was delayed until the nineteenth century. Then demand increased rapidly and transport improved greatly as a result of first canal and then railway construction. Following the initial enterprises in the immediate vicinity of Nottingham, the main centre was in the Erewash Valley where the output showed some fluctuations but in general saw a steady if unspectacular rise in the first half of the nineteenth century. Thereafter the pace quickened with the opening of much bigger pits in the Leen Valley in the 1860s and 1870s, with the Mansfield area not coming on stream until the 1890s. Production then expanded quite markedly, more than doubling between 1874 and 1890 and then rising by a further 67% by 1914. The total workforce meanwhile expanded from 12,228 in 1874 to an impressive 41,020 at the outbreak of the First World War. Moreover the growth produced an atmosphere of well being. 'Despite temporary set-backs, the mining community of the second half of the nineteenth century exuded Victorian optimism. Miners and mine owners were becoming increasingly prosperous in an increasingly prosperous world. There seemed no reason to doubt that this trend would continue indefinitely into the twentieth century'.[1] Within this broadly expansionist and optimistic scenario, some particular aspects of the coalfield's economic and social structure should be clarified. These are:

the organisation of the industry, the character of the social relationships, and the pattern of industrial relations.

While it is certainly true, as has already been pointed out, that the story of the field in this period is one of steady progress with output and labour force both expanding, at the same time there was a significant loss of productivity. Output per man, whether in terms of numbers working underground or the total workforce, peaked in the 1880s and thereafter there was a steady though not unremitting trend downwards. By the outbreak of war in 1914 for underground workers, the level had fallen by as much as 21% in the space of a quarter of a century.[2] It is then clear that the Nottinghamshire coal-mining industry was essentially a 'pick and shovel' operation with a reliance on the crude method of employing more labour to get the coal. However in the decade or so before 1914 there were attempts to raise productivity by the introduction of power-driven machinery into the pits both for the cutting and the hauling of coal. It should not be too readily assumed that the county coal-owners were unthinking reactionaries opposed to technological change. Indeed, in many respects and in comparison with some other districts the innovatory record of many companies was quite impressive. Equally it is true to say that, as far as mechanical coal cutters were concerned, the geological conditions were not always favourable and their introduction could, as we shall see, be a potent cause of industrial unrest.[3]

One other particular feature of the production organisation of the coalfield needs to be emphasised, and that is the widespread prevalence of the butty or contracting system. By the second half of the nineteenth century, the original arrangement whereby a whole pit was leased to a contractor, or more usually two contractors, had been much modified. Mining was becoming more complex and capital intensive with more extensive operations and the problem of effective control was more crucial. Thus the so-called 'big' butty gave way to the 'little' butty. Now he was quite clearly under the supervision of officials increasingly often with technical and professional qualifications, appointed by the employing company. The butty's responsibility thus shrank to that merely of getting the coal from one working area or stall where he was responsible for paying the men working in his team.[4]

Yet although the butties had become emasculated in their position in the production process, both their history and continued existence may be said to have had profound effects on the region's social relationships. Generally speaking there was a significant distance between them and other miners and the different social status was marked in a number of ways. Not surprisingly there was a differential in income which exhibited itself most notably in that butties often lived in rather more substantial houses. Even more obvious was the tendency to worship apart from other miners, very often in the Congregational Chapel which, in a number of Nottinghamshire villages became known locally as 'the butty's lump'. Furthermore it has to be realised that, as 'little butties', this group formed a not inconsiderable number and thus made up an important stratum of local society.[5]

The likely effects of the butties' higher social status on the development of working-class politics and more specifically the nature of industrial relations was a potential for uncertainty and even incoherence rather than the solidarity traditionally ascribed to coal-mining communities. Furthermore, in this respect it has to be remembered that many Nottinghamshire pit villages and towns had been in existence with their local economies based on agriculture, and textiles before the great expansion of coal in the nineteenth century. Different communities thus 'acquired different and overlapping traditions, different senses of their local order'. Moreover, it has been argued that the rapid urbanisation of parts of the county and especially the almost 'suburbanisation' effect of the expansion of Nottingham had a significant effect on the developing attitudes of the inhabitants of the coalfield.[6]

Finally, in considering the social structure it is necessary to draw special attention to the influential role the colliery owners sought to play in the community and this was often the result of a generally paternalistic attitude adopted by some employers towards their workforce. In some cases certainly it could be seen as an attempt to assume the mantle hitherto worn by the gentry and aristocracy. Sometimes such employers had themselves come from the minor landed class. Sometimes there was conflict between old and new as for example most prominently at Hucknall where the colliery owner J.E. Ellis did battle with the Duke of Portland for control of the town. Ellis was a particularly striking example of employer paternalism in the Nottinghamshire coal industry and the extent of his benevolence both towards his employees and the community as a whole was truly proverbial. His outlook on industrial relations was influenced by two overriding principles: the importance of personal contacts and a belief in conciliation as the only sure way to resolve conflict. Moreover these principles were clearly demonstrated by his concern to maintain regular and on-going cooperation with his employees' trade union. In the wider community he supported the chapels, became involved in education and served as chairman for a period of the local Board of Health. Ultimately he pursued his concept of service into national politics, becoming a Liberal MP in 1884, though still by no means severing his local interests. Unusual in the degree and intensity of his activity perhaps, but in its very essence, Ellis was by no means alone amongst the class of Nottinghamshire colliery owners in this period. It would however be true to say that, on balance, conditions of work and industrial relations were rather better in the Leen Valley pits than in the Erewash Valley. This was to become more marked when, as a result of the 1893 lock-out, the Leen owners, with Ellis and two other enlightened proprietors, Thomas Bayley and Colonel C. Seely at the head, broke away to form a separate owners' association.[7]

In view of what has been said so far, it is then not surprising that the character of industrial relations was comparatively even tempered although this is not to deny that there were episodes of conflict which sometimes engendered a good deal of bitterness. It is however perfectly true to say that the officials of the county miners' union, the Nottinghamshire Miners Association (NMA) had from its inception in 1881 followed a policy of cautious moderation.[8] Some of this might be put down to the strong Methodist/Liberal influence which permeated the union and certainly was demonstrated by the case of William Bailey who led the body, variously acting as Secretary or Agent during much of the formative period of its history (1887-1896). He was succeeded by J.G. Hancock who served under him for a short period as Assistant Secretary before assuming the leader's role as Agent, a post he held from 1897 to 1914. While views of Bailey seem to be marked by a good deal of warmth and regard for his services to the NMA, 'J.G.', as we will see, was to pursue a career which evoked considerable controversy.[9] Just as important as personality as a factor in the association's fundamental moderation was the elaborate procedure written into the rules to implement strike action. Not only was the approval of the governing council required before a strike ballot could be taken, but further checks were built into the process so that it could take as long as three months before a strike was declared 'official'. And of course during that period, the union's officials were busy exploring all of the possibilities for a negotiated settlement of the dispute in question.[10]

As with almost all unions the NMA had a good deal of difficulty in establishing itself.[11] As one of the founder members of the national body, the Miners' Federation of Great Britain (MFGB), it had been keen to secure total union membership of the county's workforce. This aim of a 'closed shop' was consistently followed by the leadership and excellent progress was made towards the ideal in the last decade of the nineteenth century. However in the years before the First World War there still remained a significant proportion (between 13 and 20%) of the workforce outside the association's ambit.[12] Still, the fact remains that by the beginning of the present century the NMA had much to feel satisfied about. With a rising membership it had now secured recognition from all the colliery owners in the county. Further evidence of respectability was the acquisition of new offices and houses for its permanent officials while in 1906 it introduced a retired miners pension scheme which compared very favourably with the modest state payment initiated in 1908. Admittedly there were some internal tensions: between the pits in the Leen and those in the Erewash valley; between butties and other miners; and between those who were politically Lib-Lab and those who sought independent representatives. But these difficulties did not seem to be critical or even irreconcilable given the prevailing tone of moderation.[13]

Yet a policy of caution and moderation was far from producing a body that was supine or inert and throughout the period of its growth and maturity, from the mid 1890s to the end of the First World War, the NMA was constantly engaged in a battle to protect its members' interests. On several occasions this resulted in conflicts at individual collieries which could be both protracted in terms of time, and extensive in terms of the number of men involved.[14] Moreover in 1893 the union was involved, along with the rest of the MFGB, in the Great Lock-Out arising from the owners' attempts to secure large wage reductions in the face of a marked, albeit temporary, fall in demand. Throughout the fifteen week dispute the men's resolve held up remarkably well, buoyed up no doubt by expressions of support not only from the public as a whole but also from some of the colliery owners themselves. While it is not appropriate to go into the details here it is important to notice how the main results affected the NMA.[15] Undoubtedly there was a general feeling of euphoria when the terms of the settlement were announced, 'the unionists ... their wives and their friends thronged the streets and public places [of the mining villages] where their enthusiasm ran riot'.[16] Despite some misgivings expressed about the working of the newly established Conciliation Board,[17] by and large the settlement of the wages issue was by no means unsatisfactory. Wage rates henceforth were negotiated on two elements: the basic rate, to be determined locally and being very much dependent on conditions from pit to pit; and an additional percentage to be negotiated through the MFGB. Otherwise the union recovered its strength very rapidly: by the end of 1895 it had cleared all the debts incurred as a result of payments made to members, and although there was a reduction in membership which took rather longer to recoup, by the end of the century numbers had recovered not only in absolute numerical terms but also in percentage relationship to the total workforce in the county's pits.

For the ensuing years the story is one of frequent local disputes which kept the union's leadership very busy while still concerned to preach caution and moderation.[18] In spite, or perhaps because of the 1893 settlement, disputes over wages were extremely frequent at individual collieries and on occasions there were strikes lasting several weeks at Pinxton (1898), Radford (twice in 1905) and Trowell Moor (1906-7). Trouble over the rates paid to boys was also common notably because pay was low and sometimes there was no proper price list. If such disputes went to strike action, it might well be unofficial and could lead to considerable disruption. Thus, we find the Leen Valley Owners Association writing to the NMA on 2 July 1910 complaining about the frequency of such action and its effect on the workforce as a whole.[19]

The utilisation of coal-cutting machinery was also a cause of trouble and again could lead to long drawn out conflict. The introduction of such machinery at Sutton in 1896 resulted in something like two years of unrest and there was a three month strike over this issue at Brierley Hill in the late Summer/Autumn of 1902. Trouble at Radford in 1908 was followed by a notably bitter dispute at Clifton which lasted over a year before being settled by arbitration. Attempts to enforce the MFGB agreed policy of the closed shop caused strikes lasting respectively ten days at Trowell Moor in April 1901 and two months at Newstead in 1905. Other issues which created tensions included the use of safety lamps, demands for shovel rather than fork/screen coal filling and the provision of meal breaks for boys arising from the 1908 Coal Mines Act. Nor does it seem as if this evidence of a degree of unrest in the industrial relations of the mining industry is at all unusual for the time. If one pauses to look for a moment at the rather more broadly based regional picture presented by the Board of Trade figures for strikes and lockouts in the North and West Midlands for the years 1898-1910,

the comparison is instructive. Thus in three separate years —
1901, 1909 and 1910 — the number of individual disputes
topped 200 and in only one year, 1906, did it fall below 100 to
96. In terms of actual numbers involved, the peak years were
1902, with 62,705 workers and 1909 with 61,745 and in four
other years the numbers ranged between 23,915 (1898) and
39,693 (1900). Only the period between 1903 and 1907 could
really be regarded as 'quiet' in terms of industrial relations.[20]
Moreover, returning to the situation in Nottinghamshire, it
does appear that, in many cases, the NMA did indeed succeed
in resolving the disputes without recourse to open confronta-
tion.

Finally, in the period immediately before the outbreak of
war the union's attention was concentrated on two matters:
the settlement of surface worker's wages and the involvement
in the MFGB agitation on the Minimum Wage/Abnormal
Conditions issue. In the former, purely local case, the NMA
negotiated an agreement with the employers on 24 March
1912 on the wages paid both to boys and adults, but although
the settlement encompassed considerable improvements there
were two blemishes. In the first instance the agreement did
not cover the Enginemen and Firemen whose grievances were
of long-standing and who had to wait until the end of the year
before completion. Furthermore the settlement still did little
or nothing to eradicate the long-standing differential between
the Leen and Erewash Valley rates. The NMA Council clearly
felt sufficiently uneasy about the Erewash men's disadvan-
tage to comment that 'this must not be regarded as an
admission by us that wages should be below those prices in
the Leen Valley'.[21]

However, serious as this was it paled into insignificance
beside the other issue of 1912, the Minimum Wage Agitation
leading to the second great pit stoppage of the period. It is not
necessary to go into all of the details of this conflict, except to
indicate how the matter affected Nottinghamshire miners
and their union.[22] The underlying issue arose from the
difficulties which coal face workers on contract inevitably
faced whenever their earnings were reduced because unex-
pectedly adverse conditions slowed down the rate of coal

getting. This problem had been generally recognised for some time and the custom had grown up of so-called 'consideration payments' to meet any possible shortfall. There had been problems of interpretation as to what constituted 'abnormal conditions' and this was exacerbated in the early years of the twentieth century by companies, anxious to reduce costs, looking very hard at such payments. The matter was sufficiently critical for the MFGB to pick it up and carry at its 1910 national conference a resolution calling for 'a fair living wage to be paid to all miners working in abnormal places', and a national agitation for a 'minimum' wage was launched. Trouble now escalated rapidly, the flashpoint coming in South Wales where there was a long drawn out strike involving some violence, notably at Tonypandy in November 1910. The issue quickly became a focal point for the growing Syndicalist movement and, although the MFGB took up the cause, the militant were dissatisfied with the extent of the support with the result that the Federation was riven by ideological conflict.[23] However the national body Executive's predilection for a mediated settlement based on local district agreements was reversed when an approach to the owners failed to produce an acceptable response (29 September 1911). Hence at the national conference on 6 October 'the general principle of the minimum wage was for the first time affirmed as the most urgent aim of the Federation' and it was agreed to pursue this on a national basis.[24] A further equivocal response from the owners triggered the final breakdown. A national ballot approved strike action and a six week strike ensued, commencing 1 March 1912, involving something like one million men, 'a coal stoppage of a magnitude hitherto unknown in any country'.[25] Moreover it was a stoppage that could only be resolved by government intervention leading to legislation, the 1912 Minimum Wage Act.[26]

It is not unfair to say that, throughout this episode, the reactions of Nottinghamshire miners were somewhat muted. Initially, it would appear perhaps that the issue of 'abnormal places' was less of a problem in the county than in some other districts.[27] Moreover the rates generally recognised in Nottinghamshire were well in excess of the five shillings per week

figure fixed by the MFGB. Thus, when the vote was taken for
strike action, although the county as a whole voted strongly
in favour (17,086 for the strike and 5,386 against) it is notable
that the majority was somewhat below the 4:1 average for the
Federation as a whole and certainly well below the enthusiasm recorded in South Wales and Yorkshire.   Of equal
significance perhaps was the number who failed to vote: as far
as can be ascertained, some 30% of the registered membership. When a second ballot was held at the end for prolonging
the strike, there was now a very narrow majority for carrying
on and the percentage of abstainers was over 50%. Throughout, the newspapers had commented on the 'friendly' atmosphere and there had been an opportunity for the newly elected
president of the NMA, George Spencer, to reinforce the
union's traditional moderation by calling on the men to act
'peaceably'.[28]   In fact there seems to have been a general
perception that Nottinghamshire was not going to gain anything whatever the outcome. This was to be amply reinforced
in the final outcome.   While establishing the principle of a
national minimum wage, the 1912 Act which had ended the
conflict had, in fact, left the actual wage levels to be negotiated
on a local basis by specially established Joint District Boards
composed of representatives of both sides of the industry
under a neutral chairman.   In the case of Nottinghamshire,
and indeed many other districts, agreement proved impossible and a figure was in effect imposed by the chairman. The
award, as well as being resented as arbitration by the back
door, was generally seen as being pointless.   One reported
comment summed up the affair thus: 'We came out for
nothing and we are going back for the same'.   Hancock felt
that, in the circumstances, it was the best they could get but
inevitably some of the resentment boiled over on to the
union's officials. Hence, Spencer is found plaintively bewail-
ing that they were being subjected to 'blasphemy and slander
of the darkest and deepest degree'.[29]

Apart from its prime and ongoing concern for industrial
relations, the NMA, like most of the other district mining
associations, found itself drawn increasingly into politics.

However, its path turned out rather differently from many of its MFGB colleagues. The marked liberal leanings of the NMA had been noticeable from its earliest years in existence and were not initially unusual.[30] Bailey had been a committed Lib-Lab and was on terms of close personal friendship with J.E. Ellis who took the chair at the union's first annual demonstration. Two other Liberal coal owners, Thomas Bayley of the Digby Colliery Company and Colonel C. Seely of the Babbington pits had also been prominent in their assistance.[31] Inevitably there had been general support for the parliamentary ambitions of the owners and, at local level, the NMA had given its backing to the Lib-Lab candidature of William Mellors in the first county council election in 1889. At the same time however, under Bailey, the union had by no means distanced itself from the developing idea of independent Labour representation and had been quite happy to host Tom Mann at its 1889 demonstration and Keir Hardie at the one held in 1892.

However, under J.G. Hancock the commitment to Liberalism became more pronounced, especially as the issue of independent Labour representation became even more urgent following the formation of the Labour Representation Committee (fore-runner of the Labour Party) in 1900. In that very year, Hancock invited the Liberal politician A.B. Markham, one of the most prominent colliery owners in the East Midlands, and MP for Mansfield, to be present at the opening of the union's new offices in Basford.[32] In 1906, on the occasion of the general election, the NMA Council, on Hancock's prompting, sent out a request that all lodges should act as canvassing organisations for Liberal candidates.[33] Nor was any of this apparently much at variance with grass-roots opinion, at least insofar as this is indicated by the outcome of the ballots organised by the MFGB on the issue of affiliation to the newly emergent Labour Party. In the ballot of 1906 the majority of NMA members against was in the ratio of 6:1 while in 1908 although the proportion in favour was significantly increased, only just over 20% of the total membership bothered even to record their preference.

Hancock, however, was to find his undoubted and growing predilection for Liberalism increasingly difficult to sustain, given the fact that, despite the Nottinghamshire vote, the
MFGB as a whole had voted for affiliation. As a result, all the
Federation's MPs and candidates were required to sign the
Labour Party's constitution, thus presenting the NMA's leader
with an awkward dilemma. Nor was the crunch long delayed. In 1909 the constituency of Mid-Derbyshire fell vacant
and, since the Derbyshire Miners Association had no suitable
candidate, it was agreed that Hancock should run. There then
followed an extraordinary sequence of events in which
Hancock, turning first one way and then the other, attempted
to ride both Labour and Liberal horses to the mounting
irritation of both parties. However, the balancing act became
ever more difficult to sustain and inevitably Hancock's true
sympathies became crystal clear; in Arthur Markham's un-
consciously ironic phrase he was 'a straight-forward, simple
minded Liberal'.[34] Whatever else one might have called J.G.,
'simple-minded' does not quite seem appropriate. Yet with
the support of both the NMA and its opposite number in
Derbyshire he hung on until 1914 when the MFGB finally
disowned him. But within the NMA he maintained his
position and, with the support of the new president, George
Spencer, he sought to strengthen it. Thus, in 1912, at their
prompting the Council refused to allow a proposal for the
candidature of Bob Smillie, the MFGB vice-president no less,
in the Nottingham West constituency. Then they proposed
that the NMA should actually secede from the Federation's
political fund and this final manoeuvre was only frustrated
after a lengthy and bitter campaign mounted by a well
organised radical group within the union. The episode is
notable not only for the light it casts on the NMA's leadership
but also because it saw the formulation of a programme for
action counter to the traditional moderation which had hitherto marked the association's policies. In addition of course
it foreshadowed the divisions within the union which were to
lead ultimately to George Spencer's breakaway movement
after the 1926 strike.[35]

Such then were the main features of the scene in the Nottinghamshire coalfield before 1914. While the detail of the reality is undoubtedly complex, equally there are a number of features which come over quite clearly and which need to be borne in mind in the detailed analysis of events in Eastwood. In the first place, the industry was undoubtedly prospering and, although there were some setbacks, in general the figures indicate strong, underlying progress measured in terms of production and wage levels. This in turn seems to have engendered an underlying spirit of optimism which was shared by both sides of industry. On the employers' side there seems to have been a concern to establish good relationships with their workforce and that this could, at least in some cases, result in attitudes and actions characteristic of paternalism. In their efforts to make their industry more productive, they seem to have been at least marginally ahead of their fellow owners in other parts of the United Kingdom, at least in the crucial matter of installing coal-cutting machinery. On the other side the county union sought to establish both a moderate and conciliatory tone in its conduct of industrial relations but also, in political terms remained wedded to the notion of Lib-Labism even after the rest of the MFGB had moved across to Labour. No doubt the NMA's stance reflected the fact that it represented a constituency which was very far from being the traditional solidary mining workforce. The existence of a significant stratum of butties within the mining community contributed to that but so too, according to recent research, did the fact that Nottinghamshire pit communities were not, by and large, closed, homogeneous entities but were shaped by a number of differing social traditions. The 'moderate' leadership thus represented a 'moderate' membership, although in no way did moderation mean that men were not prepared to contest for improvements in terms of wages and conditions. For all sorts of reasons the years before the outbreak of war in 1914 seem to have been generally a period of industrial tension and conflict and, as has been made clear above, the Nottinghamshire coalfield seems to have shared in this unrest.[36]

References

1.   A. R. Griffin, *Mining in the East Midlands 1550-1947* (Frank
      Cass, 1971), p. 119 and the tables on pp. 119-20, 121. For the
      general historical details see the same work, especially part
      II chapters I and IV.

2.   See Griffin, *Mining*. The table on pp. 119-20 gives a com-
      plete sequence of figures.

3.   Again, see Griffin, *Mining*, for an invaluable discussion of
      the issue of technological innovation. For a comparison
      with the British coal-mining industry as a whole see M. W.
      Kirby, *The British Coalmining Industry 1870-1946* (Macmillan,
      1977). N. K. Buxton, *The Economic Development of the British
      Coal Industry* (Batsford, 1978), together with the same au-
      thor's 'The Coal Industry', in G. Roderick and M. Stephens
      (eds.), *Where Did We Go Wrong? Industrial Performance Edu-
      cation and the Economy in Victorian Britain* (Falmer Press,
      1981).

4.   There is an admirably succinct description of the butty
      system in A. R. Griffin, *The Miners of Nottinghamshire, Vol.
      I, 1881-1914* (Department of Adult Education, University of
      Nottingham, 1955), pp. 137-8. Otherwise for more detail on
      its development see Griffin, *Mining*, especially pp. 28-32
      and 117-118.

5.   For a further discussion of this see D. Gilbert, *Class Commu-
      nity and Collective Action: Social Change in Two British Coal-
      fields 1850-1926* (Oxford, 1992), especially p. 157. There is
      also an interesting discussion of the nature and social
      ramifications of the butty system with special reference to
      Arthur Lawrence, D. H. Lawrence's father and himself a
      butty in the Eastwood pits of Barber Walker, in C. Holmes,
      'A Study of D. H. Lawrence's Social Origins', *Literature and
      History*, Volume 6, No. 1 Spring 1980, p. 85.

6.   Gilbert, *Class Community and Collective Action*, pp. 141-142.

7.   *Ibid.*, pp. 215-23. For the situation generally in the Leen
      Valley see Griffin, *Mining*, pp. 156-7 and 185-6.

8. A detailed history of the NMA is provided by A.R. Griffin, *The Miners of Nottinghamshire, Vol. I*, although additional reference needs to be made to Griffin, *Mining*, especially part II chs. II, III and V.

9. For example it is worth noting that Griffin went out of his way to dedicate his 1955 volume to Bailey's memory.

10. Griffin, *Miners, Vol. I*, pp. 163-4.

11. As Griffin has pointed out, in the success of any union, much depends on the favourable or otherwise economic conditions and the early years of the NMA were marked by membership fluctuations. Also it should be remembered that two earlier attempts to found unions in the county had failed. See Griffin, *Mining*, part I ch. V.

12. See the invaluable table in Griffin, *Mining*, pp. 207-8 which makes it possible to trace both the growth in membership and the proportion of unionised workers in the crucial years 1883-1910. On the importance that the MFGB leadership placed on total union membership see Ben Pickard's account of the events leading to the Federation's formation quoted in R. Page Arnot, *The Miners: A History of the Miners Federation of Great Britain 1889-1910* (Allen and Unwin, 1949), pp. 91-2.

13. Griffin, *Mining*, pp. 182-185.

14. For details see Griffin, *Miners, Vol. I*, chs. VIII and X and Griffin, *Mining*, pp. 134-42.

15. Griffin, *Mining*, pp. 148-57. For a fascinating account by a contemporary activist, Griffin, *Miners, Vol. I*, pp. 100-101. The general causes are dealt with in detail in Arnot, *The Miners: A History*, chs. VII and VIII.

16. Griffin, *Miners, Vol. I*, p. 97.

17. Thus Bailey's attack on its chairman and his complaint that the body had made a point of 'endorsing and approving every point the owners pressed for'. Quoted in Griffin, *Mining*, p. 153.

18.   For details see Griffin, *Mining,* pp. 188-92 supplemented by further treatment in Griffin, *Miners, Vol. I,* pp. 143-59.

19.   Griffin, *Miners, Vol. I,* p. 159.

20.   Figures drawn from Board of Trade, *Abstract of Labour Statistics* (HMSO, 1913), p. 160.

21.   Griffin, *Miners, Vol. I,* pp. 168-70.

22.   The matter is treated in detail in R. Page Arnot, *The Miners: Years of Struggle* (Allen and Unwin, 1953) while the impact on Nottinghamshire and the NMA is, once again, dealt with by Griffin, *Mining,* pp. 193-6 and Griffin, *Miners, Vol. I,* pp. 164-70.

23.   Arnot, *The Miners: Years of Struggle,* p. 73.

24.   *Ibid.,* pp. 80-81.

25.   *Ibid.,* p. 95.

26.   *Ibid.,* pp. 118-22 for a full discussion of the measure's significance.

27.   Griffin, *Mining,* p. 194.

28.   Griffin, *Mining,* p. 195.

29.   Griffin, *Miners, Vol. I,* p. 170.   Griffin, *Mining,* p. 196. Interestingly the proceedings of the Joint District Board are reprinted together with the final awards compared with previous average figures in Griffin, *Miners, Vol. I,* pp. 190-200.

30.   The following paragraphs are based mainly on R. Gregory, *The Miners and British Politics 1906-1914* (Oxford, 1968), especially chapter VII, and Griffin, *Mining,* pp. 197-204.

31.   Griffin, *Mining,* p. 130.

32.   Griffin, *Miners, Vol. I,* p. 146.

33.   Gregory, *The Miners and British Politics,* p. 146.

34. *Ibid.*, p. 147.

35. The opposition was led by a young activist Herbert Booth who derived much support from a small but active ILP group. For the Mid-Derbyshire by-election and the subsequent events see: Gregory pages 148-150, 153-5 and Griffin, *Mining*, pp. 199-202.

36. On the general picture see E. H. Phelps Brown, *The Growth of British Industrial Relations* (Macmillan, 1959).

1. *High Park Colliery:* scene of some of the company's early technical innovations.

2. *Moorgreen Colliery: largest of the company's collieries and the last of the Eastwood pits to stay in production.*

III

Eastwood: The Predominance of Barber Walker

In the nineteenth century Eastwood had been a small but steadily expanding mining community standing on a hill to the east of the River Erewash on the borders of Nottinghamshire and Derbyshire. Its population had roughly doubled in the first thirty to forty years of the century, although the next three decades showed a rather less dramatic expansion of some 50-60%. From 1871 however the pace picked up again and the number rose from 2,540 to reach 4,815 by the beginning of the present century. The reason for this development was quite simply the exploitation of the coal reserves in the area and in this, of course, Eastwood was little different from other small communities on either side of the Nottinghamshire/Derbyshire boundary. Here, as at Hucknall or Ilkeston, coal was either king or very close to it. Eastwood was quite manifestly a colliery community in 1914 and so too were the hamlets and settlements which adjoined it. According to one contemporary observer no less than three quarters of the male population of Eastwood proper were employed in one way or another in coal mining.[1] While this is broadly true it does give a somewhat simplistic view of the town's social composition. Thus it should be noted that previously agriculture and hosiery had figured importantly in the economy and even when coal did come to overtake all other activities, in the period 1851-1921 at the most rather less than half of the male population was directly employed in mining.[2]

If the predominant material in the economy of Eastwood was coal, the predominant organisation was the colliery company of Barber Walker. Indeed, the economic predominance was so complete that it is perfectly in order to call Eastwood a 'company town', or perhaps more accurately a 'company village'. The origins of this partnership are to be found back in the eighteenth century and in the early nineteenth century it rapidly came both to concentrate its activities in and to dominate the central section of the Erewash valley.[3] At one point in the later years of the century, the partnership was working some ten pits in and around Eastwood, but by 1900 this number had fallen to five: Brinsley and Underwood lay respectively one and two miles to the north of the town; Moorgreen and High Park were about the same distances to the north east; while Watnall well to the east was rather out on its own being in fact closer to Kimberley than to Eastwood. In the last decade of the century, the total workforce of these five pits was 2,750, being divided up as follows: Brinsley 300, Moorgreen 800, High Park 700, Watnall 500, and Underwood 450.[4] It would seem not unreasonable to assume that the majority of the men employed at the two biggest collieries were residents of Eastwood and its adjoining hamlets and if this admittedly crude approximation be accepted, then it gives some indication of the extent to which the community as a whole depended on Barber Walker.

The management of the company was most marked for the measure of responsibility the proprietorial family gave to its general managers. This is not to say that these men were largely unsupervised — indeed far from it. One opinion has it that the continued success owed a good deal to personal supervision.[5] Equally it has been suggested that the then head of the family, Thomas Barber (1843-93), died prematurely because of worry over the fate of his pits and workmen in the Great Coal Dispute of 1893.[6] Nonetheless it still remains true that a succession of exceedingly capable managers both ran the day to day affairs and had considerable influence in the formulation of longer term policy. The best documented of these is Robert Harrison who succeeded his uncle as manager in 1852, was elevated to general manager in 1854 and was to hold the position until his death in 1891.[7] His immediate

successors were Edward Lindley (1891-1905) and John W.
Fryar (1905-1915). Vivid illustration of the standing of these
men in the community is provided by the veritable scenes of
pomp and circumstance which attended Lindley's funeral in
1905, when the cortège was headed by two bands and virtually the whole town was reckoned to have turned out for the
occasion. A final touch was the sounding of the 'Last Post' and
'Reveille' over the grave by buglers from the local Lads'
Brigade.[8]

Necessarily as a result of his long reign at the top, many of
the traditions of management were established by Harrison
and this can be illustrated by reference to three areas: capital
and technical development, industrial relations and employee
welfare. In the first instance he had been especially concerned
to plough back a significant proportion of the profits into the
improvement of existing pits and the development of new
workings. At the same time he concentrated increasingly on
the five larger relatively highly capitalised pits and closed
down smaller, less economical enterprises which had been
worked as late as 1870.[9] No doubt the fact that the company
survived the setbacks of the so-called 'great depression' owed
much to this prudent policy.[10] In terms of technical innovation
Harrison also was well to the fore, being especially concerned
to promote the safety of the pits by installing efficient ventilation systems. Thus High Park colliery (opened in 1861) was
claimed to be the first in the area to introduce the new Waddle
ventilation fan.[11] Harrison himself calculated 'that there is
fresh air to every 200 or 300 yards of face' and he took
particular pride in the fact that only forty-four fatal accidents
had been suffered over a period of fourteen years: one life for
every 215,351 tons produced.[12] This concern for safety was
not of course motivated by altruistic humanity but rather a
concern for greater efficiency (as well as to meet the increasingly tighter official regulations).[13] Yet in one important
respect, Harrison remained curiously backward: he was extremely reluctant to consider the possibility of more efficient
coal getting. One of his managers, as early as 1875, had
expressed the view that coal cutting machinery was '... absolutely necessary in order to enable coal proprietors to compete

with other districts where the holing and cutting is more easily performed and where coal is got at something like half the cost.' But Harrison remained unconvinced, claiming in 1881 that although they had indeed tried out one such machine '... we could do no good at all with it.' Like most of the rest of the industry he preferred simply to rely on employing more labour to boost production.[14]

This essentially 'hard-nosed' attitude comes out clearly in his handling of industrial relations. The management structure of the Eastwood pits had of course to take into account the fact that traditionally many pits in the East Midlands counties were worked on the 'butty' or sub-contracting system.[15] Harrison at any rate made certain that the butties were very carefully supervised by three deputies in each pit, working an overlapping shift system, so that each could 'converse as to the state of the pit with the one following up'.[16] Equally the butties were carefully chosen; in each 'stall' (60-90 yards of coal face), the operation was under the charge of 'three picked men from the ranks, as careful and as experienced men as we can get'.[17] However, this concern for the quality of the supervision and control of the labour force was also marked by an intransigence that was perhaps unusual even by the standards of Harrison's own time. It goes without saying that he viewed trade unions with singular disfavour. In 1867 his anti-unionism surfaced when he dismissed a group of employees discovered in trade union activity[18] and he was reported to have offered higher wages if employees would leave the union,[19] while the early weeks of 1873 saw a long drawn-out strike, involving some violence in the collieries at Eastwood, Hill Top and Moorgreen, over his refusal to make any concession to demands for an eight hour day.[20] In 1888-9 he caused unrest among his employees by his tardiness in conceding a wage increase which had already been agreed by the other Nottinghamshire coal owners in response to pressure applied nationwide by the miners.[21] Finally, in 1890 he committed himself to the view 'that the management should refuse to negotiate with the miners' union on the grounds that a compromise would be the likely result'.[22]

Yet, at the same time it is equally true that the partnership during Harrison's years evinced a good deal of concern for the wider welfare of its employees. Again, as with safety, this was not motivated by detached humanitarianism but by calculations of business: a relatively contented man was likely to be both more amenable and more efficient. Harrison's major achievement here was to persuade the partnership, somewhat against its will, to embark on a major programme of building houses for employees in Eastwood and Greasley in the 1870s.[23] Mainly as a result of this initiative the housing stock of Eastwood was increased by over 80% in the period between 1871 and the end of the century. Moreover these dwellings were by and large superior in their provision to that of houses previously constructed although still somewhat lacking in essential services and presenting, according to some contemporaries, a rather unprepossessing aesthetic aspect.[24] This building programme would appear to have been merely the beginning for there was apparently a proposal in 1881 to acquire land to build a hospital and twelve almshouses.[25] However, the housing scheme had to be curtailed and neither hospital nor almshouses were ever built as a result of Harrison's economies to meet the depression of the late 70s.[26] Apart from housing, there is some evidence that the company had a more than peripheral interest in educational provision. Even as far back as the 1830s and 40s sums of money and heating coal had been provided for the Sunday schools operating in the area, which it was claimed 'are sufficient to give them [i.e. the children] a good, plain education'.[27] The connection was maintained when Thomas Barber was unanimously elected chairman of the newly constituted Greasley School Board in 1876,[28] but his attendance at meetings appears to have been intermittent,[29] and soon he tendered his resignation.[30] It does, however, seem likely that the firm had given some backing to an initiative in technical education which was reported by one Thomas Evans, Midland District Mines Inspector in 1879. Scientific education, Evans believed, was an important part of a miner's training as a factor in minimising accidents. Thus 'in Eastwood they have lectures in chemistry and they prepare their pupils for the South Kensington examination and some of them pass capital examinations'.[31] Finally members of the proprietorial family and the management team began to take an increasingly active role in supporting a wide range of social activities from the formation of a Lads' Brigade to the encouragement of a collieries cricket club. In particular a significant contribution was made to the Mechanics Hall, built in the 1860s: the head of the Barber family held the presidency and the company's employees were generally to be found involved in its running.[32] This side of the company's activities was indeed to develop even more under Harrison's successors and the influence of T.P. Barber (chairman 1897-1954), and it is clear that it took a considerable, if rather self congratulatory, pride in this work.

The tenor of management under Harrison's successor Lindley did not change in essentials but there were some significant changes of emphasis. In particular, it was during this period that the company began to take a direct part in the politics of the district following the reorganisation of local government and the establishment of both county and district councils. Lindley himself served on both the county council and the urban district council, and he seemed to show a much closer interest in education and youth work, notably as a manager of the British school, as vice-president of the Lads' Brigade and Cadet Corps and for his involvement with evening classes. Along with an active interest in the Mechanics Institute, he showed a keen concern for the fortunes of the cricket club. During his period too there were significant additions to the welfare system: Lindley himself was responsible for founding and running the collieries' ambulance corps and it was in 1892 that a new recreational centre was provided for the Underwood pit by the company.

The major industrial event during the period of Lindley's management was the Great Lock-Out of 1893 which affected the coal industry in general but especially the so-called 'federated' areas. The Eastwood pits came out along with the rest of the Nottinghamshire coalfield but at bottom, the company seems to have regarded this as an unfortunate aberration in its relations with its employees, caused solely by the intervention of union 'agitators' stirring up trouble first over the eight hour day and then over the proposed reduction of wages.[33] Otherwise Lindley was becoming increasingly preoccupied if not actually worried by the depletion of coal reserves and especially the high quality top hard seam. By now, only two of the five pits — High Park and Watnall — were working this coal and Lindley calculated that within twelve years it would be totally exhausted.[34] In the circumstances he recommended the company should explore the possibilities of developing new workings at Thurgaton in the Trent Valley.[35] Unfortunately this proved a disappointment, for a test bore went down well below the level where the top hard seam was expected and found nothing, or at least nothing commercially viable. In short then, Lindley's period as manager does not appear to have been entirely happy. Before he had a chance to become established, he faced a major industrial conflict which was scarcely of his making; then followed a period of several years of depressed demand which necessarily kept output low; finally there were the difficulties attendant on his attempt to secure new areas for development. Moreover it is worth noticing that Whitelock, our major source on the company's affairs, is unusually silent on Lindley's ability as a manager, at least in comparison to the effusive tone he adopts in describing the activities not only of Harrison but also Lindley's successor John Fryar and Fryar's successor, C.W. Phillips.   True, he does give credit to him for his early assessment of the need for new development, and there is much evidence that Lindley was a highly respected man in the Eastwood community, but his grip may have begun to slip towards the end of his career, almost certainly as the result of a long, painful and ultimately fatal illness.[36]

It was at this crucial stage in events that the company came under the control of a new, young and dynamic chairman, Thomas Philip Barber. In 1902 T.P. Barber, although still only 26 years of age, had already held the chairmanship of the company for some five years. He had lately returned from the

South African War where he had performed with considerable distinction, being wounded, mentioned in despatches and decorated. He had recently married and was soon to become a father. He now seems to have decided, with the encouragement of his uncle, Robert Barber (in fact the company's lawyer) that firm decisive action was needed. This took two forms. In the first place the decision was taken to pursue an option to open up a new mine at Bentley in South Yorkshire. In the second instance, when the ailing Lindley finally died in 1905 and the new venture was running into difficulties,[37] he secured a highly capable replacement as general manager in the person of John Fryar.

Viewed from any angle T.P. Barber's life and his part in shaping not only the company but also the wider community were quite remarkable. Even more than any of his predecessors he pursued a high public profile and sought to develop the role of the company beyond the merely economic. The interest and involvement in his employees' wider welfare even reached the point where the tradition grew up that the miners' children were invited to the family home, Lamb Close, every Boxing Day, there to receive an orange and a new penny piece from the butler.[38] This, however, needs to be balanced by the fact that he was also apparently very concerned to keep trespassers away from his property. Hence there is the story of the young D.H. Lawrence and a friend inadvertently wandering into the grounds of Lamb Close, confronted by an irate T.P. Barber roundly ordering them off in no uncertain terms.[39] Most notably he sought to develop a base in local politics, following the tradition established by his predecessor and extending it further. In 1904 standing as a Conservative he took over the Newthorpe seat on the Nottinghamshire County Council, previously held by his uncle and was unopposed at the election. This gives some indication of the family and company influence for, as the local press pointed out with some surprise, this was at a time of some political turmoil 'when so many seats are being contested on the ... Education Act'.[40] In 1907 he retained his seat with a massive 70% of the turn-out when someone had the temerity to challenge him and in 1910 and 1913 on both occasions again he was given a clear run. This was merely the beginning of a long, uninterrupted career of over sixty years on the county council, during which he was variously chairman of the major committees as well as holding the chair of the whole council. That the power thus wielded was considerable there can be little doubt, although, oddly, on the occasion of his funeral in 1961, the Bishop of Southwell described him as a man 'who sought no honours for himself and was far too humble to desire publicity'.[41]

But Barber's first and increasing concern was always for the company and, as we have seen, there was something of a crisis at the time of the appointment of the new general manager John Fryar. Unlike his two predecessors he was not a Nottinghamshire man but came from County Durham, although his mining experience had been gained in the East Midlands as well as North Wales and his native north east.[42] He was known particularly in Nottinghamshire for his development of the operations at Sherwood colliery Mansfield and it was this which apparently commended him to the company when it was looking for someone to clear up the mess at Bentley. He was first asked to report on the problem and this so impressed that he was then invited to assume responsibility for the boring operation which he did early in May 1905. Following Lindley's death in the same month, T.P. Barber approached him with the offer of the general managership and, after some hesitation, he accepted, taking up his duties on 15 November.[43]

Undoubtedly with Fryar, Barber Walker had acquired a man much more in the mould of Harrison, most especially in his concern for technical improvement and capital investment. It may well be that Whitelock is right in suggesting that his major achievement was at Bentley,[44] but a good deal of his effort went into the Eastwood collieries and they were to remain his base as general manager. His major problem continued to be the one already isolated by Lindley, namely the imminent exhaustion of the top hard and the need to exploit thinner, less economical seams. Indeed, Lindley's prediction was almost as precise as it could possible have been, for by 1912 only Watnall was still working the top hard and producing a mere 300 tons per day.[45] Fryar concluded that the only way to prolong the pits' profitable life was by the wholesale introduction of coal cutting machinery and powered haulage and literally within months of taking office he had embarked on a far-reaching capital development plan. This also entailed the construction of a private electrical power plant at Moorgreen to serve all the collieries and this alone cost £20,000. The system of electric haulage underground for all the collieries was finally completed during 1908-9, and at the same time, Fryar spent another £36,000 or so, purchasing 600 railway wagons for the company. He also made significant changes in the managerial team in 1906 and again in 1911, essentially bringing in younger (and presumably more vigorous and forward-looking) men and in addition creating the completely new post of Mechanical Engineer. The introduction of coal cutters began in 1907 and continued over the next four years and these machines soon proved their worth in allowing the mining of seams barely half as thick as those hitherto worked. Without these innovations, it seems doubtful whether the company could have maintained the average annual output of one million tons from the Eastwood pits which was achieved in successive years before 1914.[46] In essence Fryar had repaired the crucial omission in Harrison's technological revolution of a generation before and was indeed placing the company at the forefront of the British mining industry.

However, all things have their price and one of the major side-effects of Fryar's much needed reforms was the period of quite intense industrial conflict which disturbed the community intermittently for something like five years. It would be wrong to assume that Fryar's attitude to industrial relations was the same as Harrison's had been or that he was especially insensitive. There is some suggestion that he was in too much of a hurry,[47] but this perhaps can be explained away by the awareness of the economic pressures on him. Thus, for example, he allowed himself to speak at some length on the

gloomy prospects facing the company at what one would
have thought was the highly inappropriate setting of the
Collieries' Cricket Club meeting in May 1909,[48] Fryar certainly accepted that workmen had a right to put their point of
view. That this was indeed so is perhaps best illustrated by
an episode which occurred in 1912. The occasion was a
meeting of the Joint Conciliation Board, set up after the
passage of the Minimum Wages Act. At this meeting, reference was made to industrial troubles at Eastwood during 1910
by the employers' chief spokesman J. Piggford of Teversal,
who claimed that the dispute over wage rates had been
caused by 'malingerers'. This was immediately contested not
only by one of the union representatives but also by Fryar who
specifically dissociated himself from Piggford's remarks. He
recollected that he had offered one rate but the men '*naturally*
wanted very much higher prices' and finally a settlement was
reached because he was prepared to guarantee a certain level
of earnings. The concession was made 'not because the men
were malingering but in order to get over the difficulty and
find a way out of the dispute'. The general tenor of Fryar's
remarks lead to the conclusion that underlying his view of
industrial relations was a belief that management and men
had a commonality of interest and both had to come to terms
with harsh economic facts.[49]

Thus, by the opening decade of the present century the
economic and social dominance of Barber Walker, both company and the proprietorial family, in Eastwood was all but
complete. The partnership was by far the largest employer
and the largest rate-payer in the district and the management
was distinguished for its high degree of technical competence
coupled with a dynamic approach to the future. The concur-
rently developing commitment to the workforce's welfare in
all its aspects meant that the community was beginning to
exhibit the hallmarks of what might be called a 'company
town'. Admittedly, in some respects, the social engineering
was pragmatic, even hit and miss, and this was not to be
remedied until the company took part in the opening of the
Dukeries' coalfield in the period between the two world wars.

Here then at Harworth, was built what was believed to be the model community of Bircotes village with literally no expense spared.[50] But even before 1914 there was clear evidence of that particular type of nineteenth century paternalism which, based on the assumption of a common economic interest between master and man, believed that social investment made sound economic sense.

References

1. W. E. Hopkin, writing under pseudonym 'Anglo-Saxon', *Eastwood and Kimberley Advertiser*, 15 March 1914.

2. A.R. Griffin and C.P. Griffin, 'A Social and Economic History of Eastwood and the Nottinghamshire Mining Country', in K. Sagar (ed.), *A D.H. Lawrence Handbook* (Manchester, 1982), pp. 127 and 129 and the table on p. 157.

3. See G.C.H. Whitelock, *250 Years in Coal: The History of Barber Walker and Company Ltd* (published privately, nd). This account is fragmented and tendentious but nonetheless invaluable as providing information not otherwise readily available and also some insight into the attitudes and assumptions of the company's management. Whitelock joined the company as head surveyor of Eastwood collieries in 1916 and was to remain associated with the Barber family well after the post-war nationalisation of the pits.

4. Figures from A.R. Griffin, *The Miners of Nottinghamshire, Vol.1, 1881-1914* (Department of Adult Education, University of Nottingham, 1955), p. 95.

5. A.R. Griffin, 'The Development of Industrial Relations in the Nottinghamshire Coalfield' (Nottingham University PhD Thesis, 1963), p. 93.

6. Whitelock, *250 Years in Coal*, p. 41.

7. For details see C.P. Griffin, 'Robert Harrison: A Study in the Development of the Management Function in a Mining

Partnership' (Nottingham University BA Thesis, 1965). Reworked as an article in *Transactions of the Thoroton Society*, 1978.

8.   *Eastwood and Kimberley Advertiser*, 12 May 1905.

9.   Notably those at Cotmanhay, Eastwood and Hill Top.

10.   See Whitelock, *250 Years in Coal*, ch. XI-XIII and C.P. Griffin, 'Robert Harrison', ch. 3.

11.   C.P. Griffin, 'Robert Harrison', ch. 3 and Whitelock, *250 Years in Coal*, p. 32. High Park was very much the show-piece colliery for technological improvement and the model on which the other pits were developed. As a result output per man in the pit was markedly superior until Harrison's reform programme was completed. See C. P. Griffin, 'An Industrial Revolution in the East Midlands Coalfields between c.1850 and c.1880? The case of the High Park Superpit', *Transactions of the Thoroton Society*, vol XCIV, 1990.

12.   Robert Harrison: evidence to *Royal Commission on Mining Accidents*, 25 November 1879, 9558. He also produced comparable figures which showed for the Midland Counties, one life for 148,867 tons and for the British coal industry as a whole, one life for 112,506 tons.

13.   C.P. Griffin, 'Robert Harrison', ch 2.

14.   C.P. Griffin, 'An Industrial Revolution', *Transactions of the Thoroton Society*, 1990.

15.   See section II.

16.   Robert Harrison: evidence to 1879 Royal Commission.

17.   *Ibid.*

18.   A.R. Griffin, *Miners, Vol. I* (1955), p. 14.

19.   A.R. Griffin, *Mining in the East Midlands 1550-1947* (Frank Cass, 1971), p. 81.

20.   *Ibid.*, p. 72 and J. E. Williams, *The Derbyshire Miners* (Allen

and Unwin, 1962), p. 132.

21. A.R. Griffin, 'The Development of Industrial Relations', p. 264.

22. C.P. Griffin, 'Robert Harrison', Introduction, p. iii.

23. *Ibid.*, ch 6.

24. Griffin and Griffin, *A Social and Economic History of Eastwood*, pp. 135-41.

25. *Kelly's Directory*, 1881.

26. C. P. Griffin, 'Robert Harrison', p. 51.

27. Evidence of Robert Harrison the elder (uncle of Robert Harrison) described as 'overlooker' of Barber Walker's collieries, *Report of Children's Employment Commission (Mines)*, February-August 1842: appendix to final report, Part II.

28. Greasley School Board Minutes, 4 May 1876.

29. See record in Minute Book 1876-7. In his absence, William Weston, one of the company's senior officials under Harrison, generally deputised.

30. Greasley School Board Minutes, 3 July 1877.

31. Evidence to *Royal Commission on Mining Accidents,* 23 April 1879.

32. See *White's, Morris'* and *Kelly's* Directories, also Whitelock, *250 Years in Coal*, pp. 71-2.

33. See Whitelock, *250 Years In Coal,* pp. 40-1.

34. See his report for 1896 quoted in Whitelock, *250 Years in Coal,* pp. 79-80.

35. *Ibid.*, p. 80.

36. Lindley had in fact contracted Bright's disease which certainly prevented him exercising his duties on the local

UDC. To be fair Whitelock does draw attention to this, *ibid.*, p. 83.

37.   Whitelock, pp. 82-3. The manager appointed to supervise the project proved to be incompetent and was dismissed in 1905.

38.   Harry T. Moore, *The Priest of Love: A Life of D. H. Lawrence* (Penguin Edition, 1976), pp. 34-5.

39.   Barber apparently threatened them with legal action with the words: 'I remind you that I am a JP'. Whereupon Lawrence muttered to his friend: 'He sounds to me like a BF'. See Moore, *The Priest of Love*, p. 52 and E. Delavenay, *D. H. Lawrence: The Man and His Work* (Heinemann, 1972).

40.   *Eastwood and Kimberley Advertiser*, 26 February 1904.

41.   *Nottingham Guardian Journal*, 19 July 1961.

42.   Whitelock, *250 Years in Coal*, p. 229, and obituary in *Nottingham Evening News*, 20 August 1915.

43.   Whitelock, *250 Years in Coal*, p. 83.

44.   *Ibid.*, p. 229.

45.   *Ibid.*, p. 49.

46.   *Ibid.*, pp. 43-4, 47, 49.

47.   See Whitelock's remark, *ibid.*, p. 47, that he 'allowed a few months to elapse to enable workmen to accustom themselves to the new conditions' before pressing on with the next phase.

48.   *Advertiser*, 7 May 1909.

49.   Proceedings of Joint District Board for Nottinghamshire 29 April 1912. Reproduced in A.R. Griffin, *The Miners of Nottinghamshire, Vol. I*, p. 190.

50.   For details of this see Whitelock, *250 Years in Coal*, especially chapters XIX and XX. For a general discussion of the

community building which was to be a prominent feature of the development of the Dukeries field see R. J. Waller, *The Dukeries Transformed: The Social and Political Development of a Twentieth Century Coalfield* (Oxford University Press, 1983).

3. *T.P. Barber, Chairman of Barber Walker from 1897.* A man of considerable economic, social and political influence in the community.

4. *W.E. (Willie) Hopkin.* A powerful source of radical ideas and comment, pictured here (right) in a later photograph with his lifelong friend, D.H. Lawrence.

IV

The Politics of the Mining Community

Evidence of the level of industrial consciousness in the Barber Walker pits and the local community before 1900 is extremely sketchy. On the one hand we have reports that by 1892 'practically all the men and boys employed at Moorgreen, Watnall, Underwood and Brinsley' were members of the union.[1] Equally when the great dispute of 1893 disrupted the coalfields, the Eastwood district pits were affected along with the rest of the county. On the other hand the strength of commitment both to collective action in general and to support for the NMA in particular is called seriously into question by three pieces of evidence.

In the first place, Watnall pit apparently ignored the union's instructions to take the 'spring holiday' in 1892.[2] Secondly in the MFGB's September 1893 ballot on the employers' proposal to reduce wages, as far as can be ascertained the percentage of men voting on the union line was relatively low, especially in the case of Watnall, and certainly in comparison with the results recorded at the pits at the north end of the Erewash Valley.[3] Finally, in 1899, the NMA Council was apparently so concerned by the large number of non-members in the Eastwood area, that it made the special appointment of John Goddard as recruiting agent and dues collector. Goddard was apparently quite successful for in his first six months in the job he enrolled 300 members.[4] But we get further hints of official union concern on the matter in the next few years. For example, between July 1905 and August 1907, no less a person in the hierarchy than J.G. Hancock, twice addressed sizeable meetings in Eastwood on the benefits of union membership[5] and in July and August 1907 he made an unsuccessful attempt to pressurise Fryar into accepting the principle of the closed shop.[6] Yet while he pursued this strong line and was later to be involved in leading the disputes in the local pits, not everyone in Eastwood was convinced of his sincerity. Thus, Willie Hopkin was later to pen this blistering indictment: 'J.G. has always been a brake on the wheels of progress in his very successful attempt to politically under-study the late lamented St Paul ... Labour will never advance a single foot towards freedom as long as such invertebrates are placed in the forefront as leaders.'[7]

Hopkin himself was at the opposite end of the Labour spectrum, unusually enough given his background as the son of a small shopkeeper. Using his privileged position as a resident columnist on the local paper, he consistently preached a programme of radical progressivism, even Socialism. In his weekly column, he reveals himself as a forceful writer, often with a pungent turn of phrase and not afraid to meet contro-versy head on whether over local or national issues. His criticisms were often biting and on more than one occasion he declared that more than persuasion might be necessary to secure the profound social changes he believed to be neces-sary.[8] Yet at the same time he could make a plea for rational argument as the only true basis for politics. Thus, what was the point of boycotting a shop because of a disagreement with the owner's politics; rather the correct course of action was 'to convert him by sound reasoning and not bludgeon him into it by trying to ruin him'.[9] His over-riding concern was with the state of society and the need to work for an improvement whatever the cost. Even if it led to loss of friends and social disapproval, 'in spite of all and in spite of constant defeats, set-backs and disappointments there is the inward soul satisfac-tion, the exhilaration of the fight and the knowledge that we are doing something towards bringing the age of sweetness and light that all men long for'.[10] He was then something of a visionary and much of what he wrote would not have looked out of place in an Independent Labour Party (ILP) or Social

Democratic Federation (SDF) tract, and in fact in later years, he publicly admitted his debt to an SDF group in Nottingham of which he had been a member.[11] And there was a marked lyrical side to his nature. From 1899 onwards he was also contributing to the *Advertiser* what he called the 'Weekly Ballad' — a series of poems in which his main themes were the beauties of nature and the countryside. These hardly make great literature but they striking evidence of the man's humanity and essential breadth of outlook, also instanced by the fact that he was one of the few people in Eastwood with whom D.H. Lawrence retained any continuous contact. In short in Hopkin we have a passionate, ethical, deeply committed yet essentially balanced human being, the motivation behind whose actions is uniquely revealed to us week by week.[12]

Primarily he was concerned with the faults of his contemporary society. The system, he thought, was 'rotten';[13] it was 'visibly breaking down' and indeed only kept going by creating a large pool of unemployment to force down wages.[14] There was profound, underlying inequality and injustice: 'Today, Britain does not belong to the British but to a few of them; the rest live, work, move and have their being in their native land on sufferance.' The obvious need for change could only be met by Socialism whose basic principle he divined to be that 'the country and all in it shall belong to the whole nation and shall be used by the people and for the people.' In this new society, capability and honesty would be properly rewarded and there would be due emphasis on the brotherhood of man with 'everybody working together for the good of all ... [instead of] everybody working separately for the good of Number One.' It would, he thought, be 'the same kind of thing as obtains in Heaven'.[15] And, as for the doubters and sceptics, he dismissed their traditional arguments. Socialism was not against religion;[16] nor was it violent;[17] nor did it mean economically idiotic divisions of the country's wealth amongst the population as a whole.[18] Moreover, given 'the terrible waste caused by the present haphazard methods of individualistic competition ... there must be a better way of doing things'.[19] As for the Liberal government and politicians, despite their promises of reform, they would, he felt, be just as evasive as any other government, given the chance. Of their proposals for old age pensions, he warned 'we shall pay for them ourselves if they can so arrange it'[20] and he was witheringly scornful of later claims that the National Insurance scheme provided a new 'Heaven on earth' for the workers.[21] Neither did he have much time for the alumni of the cabinet: Asquith and Lloyd George he found especially hard to stomach, Churchill he parodied as 'the ineffable Winston'[22] and John Burns was lashed for 'going back on pretty nearly everything he ever professed'.[23]

On the local scene he was especially critical of the way the town had been administered in the past. He refers somewhat obscurely but very pertinently, to the failure to encourage new industry into a community dangerously reliant on a single employer.[24] On education his position was rather more equivocal, although it would be true to say that he was considerably ahead of his time in advocating secondary education for all[25] and fundamentally rested his hopes for a better world on a generally improved educational system.[26]

Enough has been said now to convey the general tenor of Hopkin's contributions to the pre-1914 *Advertiser*, and it is undoubtedly true that Eastwood responded in some sense to this programme. That this was indeed so was made abundantly clear in 1905 when in March he stood for election to the UDC and not only succeeded but actually came second in the list to Edward Lindley. Furthermore, when Lindley died some six weeks later, Hopkin succeeded in securing the former's vacant county council seat.[27] He subsequently reported his first impressions of that body in a piece in the local press, arguing 'that it would be to the advantage of the council if more working men were members and there were fewer military men and members of the privileged classes'.[28]

Yet Hopkin could hardly be said to have opened the door to a new era in spite of his writings and his own personal, political success. There was no general surge of political consciousness. Merely in terms of the people elected to the council there is the oddity that although the majority of

Eastwood's inhabitants were miners, their representation on the council was minimal and was to remain so for the whole pre-1914 period.[29] Initially when the district council came into existence there does seem to have been a response from the mining community in so far as at the meeting to elect the parish council in March 1896, of the twenty-three nominees, eight were described as miners and four were in fact elected: Thomas Ball, Thomas Fulwood, Robert Hazeldine and Frederick Twigger.[30] In the elections in the Autumn of the same year, following the upgrading to urban district status, Ball, Fulwood and Hazeldine retained their places and also secured re-election in 1899.[31] This was reasonable — although of course no true reflection of the numbers in the town — but from then onwards the situation began to deteriorate. At the 1902 elections, Ball and Fulwood were the only people on the council list it is possible to identify absolutely positively as miners and at the elections of 1905 only Ball was returned. However, a certain Raistrick Waterhouse, who narrowly failed to secure election after a recount, was in fact co-opted on to the council shortly afterwards, following the death of Edward Lindley.[32] Thereafter it was a sorry tale, especially the 1908 result which, one might reasonably have expected to reflect the industrial conflict described below. Of the twenty-seven candidates, six were miners including Ball, William Goodwin of High Park colliery and Thomas Carlin of Moorgreen. Both Goodwin and Carlin can be positively identified as members of the Eastwood Central Committee and, moreover, the NMA executive had agreed to make a contribution to their election expenses.[33] In the event only Ball was elected and of the last six places on the voting list, five were taken by the other miners' candidates who between them polled a mere 15% of the popular vote.[34] 1911 saw a similar fiasco, with only three candidates, two coming bottom of the poll and well adrift of the rest, although the indestructible Ball still retained his seat.

Indeed, it may well be the above developments that help explain the non-emergence of a truly politically conscious spirit among the Eastwood miners. Ball was clearly a man of

standing and prestige in the community but he represented
a very different tradition of working-class activity than that
advocated by Hopkin. Some brief consideration of his background may reinforce the point. Thomas Ball was not by birth
an Eastwood man, coming from Derbyshire where he began
his working life as a miner before moving to the town in 1876
at the age of 21.[35]   The family was staunchly Primitive
Methodist and Ball involved himself in chapel work to such
an extent that he served as a Sunday School teacher for nearly
forty years, ran a Young Men's class for thirty of those years,
and was for some time secretary of the Kimberley PM circuit.
Not surprisingly his religion combined a commitment to
temperance and he also served as secretary of the Eastwood
Band of Hope. In local politics, he first became prominent in
the community's opposition to an attempt by the Basford
Board of Guardians to force the town to provide itself with an
efficient fire engine.[36]   In 1886 he was elected to the Burial
Board[37] and later served as an Overseer of the Poor.[38] As we
have already seen he was to be an ever present member of the
parish council and the successor body, the Urban District
Council. It would appear that, in terms of party allegiance,
Ball was a Liberal but the whole tenor of his life and his
achievement in the community certainly did not predispose
him to any radical collectivist view of society. Although he
took part in the industrial conflict which will be described
below, his chief contribution was the organisation of the relief
of the resulting distress among the miners' families. This he
was to refer to, somewhat self consciously perhaps, as 'the
Christ-like work... in hand'.[39] The phrase sums up his attitude
most nearly in that, for him, religious and moral imperatives
were separate from and more important than socio-political
considerations. Certainly he chimed in well with the indus-
trially moderate, politically Lib-Lab tone which J.G. Hancock
and other prominent members of the NMA were assiduously
seeking to maintain.

Of even greater significance perhaps was the man who
was elected to the UDC along with Ball in 1914, one Joseph
Birkin. Birkin was in fact one of the 'butties' who were already

prominent in local circles of the NMA and the extent of his following can be gauged by the fact that, in the election, he came out ahead of Ball, Hopkin and a number of other well-established dignitaries.[40] He was a man of strong personality and wide-ranging interests, having something of a reputation as a violinist and running his own orchestra as a sideline. Significantly he described himself as an 'independent' but he was to achieve more lasting fame (or notoriety) as the leader of the group which was influential in persuading George Spencer to start his breakaway from the NMA in 1926.[41]

It would seem then, that in terms of political consciousness, Ball and Birkin were far more representative of the general tenor of Eastwood opinion and attitudes than was the radical Hopkin. Both eschewed the notion of conflict, albeit in their different ways, one looking back to a nineteenth century tradition of acceptance of the employer's power, the other looking forward to more active co-operation based on common interest. Of the general lack of political consciousness there is one further fragment of evidence which may be significant. In the Spring and Summer of 1910 the ILP organised a series of Sunday morning meetings in Eastwood but while these were all publicised in the local press[42] there is no report of any of the meetings. Either they did not take place, or were so poorly attended that the editor did not deem them newsworthy. Whatever the reason, perhaps this is a significant straw in the wind and tells us most of what we need to know about the Eastwood mining community's collective state of mind in this critical period in the area's economic and social history.

References

1.   A.R. Griffin, *The Miners of Nottinghamshire, Vol. I* (Department of Adult Education, University of Nottingham, 1955), p. 78.

2.   This was the traditional union reaction to try and preserve

jobs and wages when a glut of coal threatened market prices. All the other four pits apparently fell into line, according to a list printed by the *Nottingham Guardian*, Griffin, *Miners, Vol. I*, p. 86.

3.   See tables reproduced by Griffin, *Miners, Vol. I*, pp. 95 and 99:

	Men employed	Number voting for union recommendation
Brinsley	300	145
Underwood	450	251
New Watnall	500	127-130
Moorgreen	800	435
High Park	700	424-452

Compare these figures with returns from the large pits further up the valley, which incidentally were still 'out' when the others returned to work in October:

Pye Hill	1050	857-900
Pinxton	1000	721-745

4.   Griffin, *Miners, Vol. I*, p. 143.

5.   *Kimberley and Eastwood Advertiser*, 7 July 1905 and 2 November 1906.

6.   *Advertiser*, 26 July and 9 August 1907.

7.   W.E. Hopkin, writing under the pseudonym 'Anglo-Saxon' *Advertiser*, 5 September 1913.

8.   *Advertiser*, 13 December 1907 and 27 October 1911 as examples.

9.   *Advertiser*, 7 February 1908.

10.   *Advertiser*, 24 January 1908.

11.   BBC Radio broadcast, 22 March 1940, entitled 'I Like to Remember'. Transcript in Hopkin Collection in Eastwood Public Library.

12. In fact to chronicle this in detail would be scarcely appropriate but it seems possible to secure an accurate indication by a restricted sampling of Hopkin's column from three critical periods: 1907-8; 1911; 1913-14.

13. *Advertiser*, 13 December 1907.

14. *Advertiser*, 27 October 1911.

15. *Advertiser*, 3 January 1908.

16. Although he did once comment: 'If the energy, time and thought wasted on what I might call the post-coffinal region had been used for the betterment of this world's conditions, we would not now be praying with lack-lustre faith 'Thy Kingdom Come' .....', *Advertiser*, 6 October 1911.

17. Thus his comment 'We would not crush a worm', *Advertiser*, 3 November 1911.

18. *Advertiser*, 3 January 1908.

19. *Advertiser*, 3 January 1908.

20. *Advertiser*, 13 December 1907. The remark is both evocative of and anticipatory of Snowden's 'servile state'.

21. *Advertiser*, 20 October 1911.

22. *Advertiser*, 27 October 1911.

23. *Advertiser.*, 14 February 1908.

24. *Advertiser*, 13 December 1908.

25. *Advertiser*, 15 August 1913.

26. *Advertiser*, 9 May 1913.

27. *Advertiser*, 7 April, 7 July 1905.

28. *Advertiser*, 4 August 1905.

29. Hopkin also made the point some time later in his 'Anglo-Saxon' column in the *Advertiser*: 'In a town like Eastwood

where three-fourth of the men are miners, there ought to be more miners elected', *Advertiser*, 15 April 1914.

30. Eastwood Parish Council Minutes, 9 March 1896 (Notts County Archives).

31. Eastwood UDC Minutes, 7 October 1896 and May 1899. (Notts County Archives).

32. See UDC Minute Book, 1902, 1905 and *Advertiser*, 7 April 1905.

33. Griffin, *Miners, Vol I*, p. 161. For the role the Eastwood Central Committee played see below: section V.

34. *Advertiser*, 20 March, 10 April 1908. UDC Minutes 1908.

35. Most of these biographical details come from an account of his life published on the occasion of his simultaneous elevation to the chairmanship of the UDC and the local bench in 1913. *Advertiser*, 25 April 1913.

36. Eastwood Vestry Minutes, 24 September 1885 (Manuscript, Notts County Archives).

37. *Ibid.*, 28 October 1886.

38. *Ibid.*, 23 March 1893.

39. *Advertiser*, 24 July 1908.

40. *Advertiser*, 20 March, 10 April 1914. See also J. E. Williams, *The Derbyshire Miners* (Allen and Unwin, 1962), pp. 676-7.

41. A.R. Griffin, *Miners, Vol II*, p. 97

42. *Advertiser*, 29 April, 13 May, 8 July, 2 September.

5. *Working Underground.*

6. *Eastwood Miner at Leisure.*

V

Industrial Conflict 1907-1912

The picture of Eastwood drawn so far does not seem especially unusual within the broader context of the Nottinghamshire coalfield. The power and influence of Barber Walker
was considerable, owing much to a management that was
both vigorous and forward-looking. For their part, the miners
seemed generally quiescent in spite of the relatively advanced
political ideas being peddled by the young radical, Willie
Hopkin, in the local press. Yet this relative calm was to be
shattered and, for more than four years, there was considerable industrial tension and conflict. During the period from
the Autumn of 1907 to the Spring of 1912, the trouble reached
a climax on three occasions: a three month strike at the
beginning of 1908; a twenty-six week lock-out affecting three
of the collieries in 1910; and the participation in the National
Minimum Wage dispute early in 1912.

The initial trouble was clearly in response to Fryar's
programme of modernisation to which reference has already
been made. All the implied and actual changes which this
entailed were probably bound to cause trouble but the main
issue came to be not so much the conditions of work as the
wage rates the general manager was offering. These were felt
to be low in comparison with other pits in the area. Tension
mounted throughout the Autumn of 1907, finally coming to
a head over the Christmas period, and on 3 January 1908 an
all-out strike commenced which was to last until March. In
considering the effect of this long, drawn-out struggle on the

development of attitudes it is possible to concentrate on three elements: the role of the NMA officials; the reaction of the four pits based on Eastwood and its adjacent communities; and the significantly different reaction of the Watnall/Kimberley men.

Throughout the dispute, Hancock, who was naturally as the NMA agent mainly responsible for the conduct of negotiations, generally advanced a fairly hard line and he was supported on occasions by other senior men in the NMA including Charles Bunfield, the holder of the presidency during 1907-8. There is no doubt that Hancock spent a good deal of time on the matter and worked hard both in stiffening his troops' resolve and negotiating with the employers and the local MP Arthur Markham who made a somewhat unfortunate attempt at mediation.

Initially on the men's part, there was an intention not only to work closely with Hancock but also to maintain a united front. Thus a mass meeting on Christmas Eve 1907 determined to leave the handling of the dispute to a newly formed Central Committee representative of all five pits. This body was to be composed of thirteen members; two from each of Watnall, Brinsley and Underwood, three from High Park and four from Moorgreen. But the degree of solidarity was not to be maintained for long: from the very first there was a marked difference in emphasis between the reactions of the Eastwood pits and the Watnall/Kimberley men and, as the strike dragged on, even more serious differences of opinion emerged to divide the former.

In Eastwood the commitment can be measured in part by the publicly demonstrated response of the men. Although the local newspaper sometimes seems to 'go over the top' in its descriptions, there is no mistaking the enthusiastic atmosphere it conveys in its reports of meetings.[1] During the third week of January 1908, a Central Relief committee was formed and perhaps even more significant of local feeling was the nature of the man who took on the duties of secretary to this body, Thomas Ball. As has already been pointed out, in no sense could Ball be described as a 'trouble-maker' or a 'radical', even less a 'socialist'.

The first signs of uncertainty among the Eastwood men
surfaced early in February and arose as the result of a singularly ill-judged intervention in the dispute by the local Liberal
MP Sir Arthur Markham. Speaking at a gathering at Beauvale
on the evening of 1 February, he claimed to have solved the
problem by meeting Hancock and Fryar earlier in the day and
prevailing on them to come to an understanding which 'will
be acceptable to every man in this district'.[2] Now this was
pure wishful thinking not to say positively misleading. In the
first place, Markham had given everyone the impression that
the meeting had been a joint affair between himself and the
two protagonists, whereas in fact, Hancock revealed in a
speech to the Eastwood men on 6 February that at no time on
1 February had he met with Fryar. Moreover, Markham's
enigmatic statement was also revealed in reality to be no more
than a proposal for arbitration based on the rates payable at
the neighbouring collieries of the Digby, Oakes and Butterley
companies. This was roundly rejected by Hancock at the same
meeting.[3] Nonetheless it seems clear that the 'Markham
proposal' caused some wavering. On the evening of 5 February the Eastwood Central Committee met for no less that three
hours before rejecting it and this decision when relayed to the
large crowd awaiting the outcome caused 'astonishment and
bitter disappointment'.[4] The wavering was however temporary for on the following day, two well attended mass meetings endorsed the committee's decision. Moreover the uncertainty seems to have led to a hardening of attitudes which was
marked by the introduction of a new element into the dispute:
the issue of non-union labour in the Barber Walker pits. It will
be remembered that Hancock had made a sustained, though
unsuccessful, attempt to enforce union membership between
1905 and 1907 and he now returned to this theme at one of the
mass meetings on 6 February, where he threatened to make
'non-union men toe the line in future' — a remark which was
apparently greeted with applause.[5] Moreover, this theme was
reinforced by a strong speech made at yet another packed
mass meeting the following week by John Goddard, the local
NMA organiser, who claimed that it was 'a surprise packet for

the company when they found how many men were in the union'.[6] The editor of the *Advertiser,* in a comment attacking the whole idea of forcing men to join a union, surmised that in fact this was now the real issue at stake rather than wage rates.[7] That this was indeed so, was shortly afterwards confirmed by the publication of correspondence between Hancock and Fryar in the period 10 to 15 February, in which the former admitted that there was virtually nothing between them on the financial issue.[8] Moreover, Hancock now apparently deemed it necessary to increase the pace still further by making at a meeting on 18 February what was notably his most aggressive speech so far. He first attacked those who had argued in favour of arbitration which he said 'is rotten and stinks in the nostrils of all trade unionists'. He then attacked Barber Walker for consistently underpaying its employees. Finally, in a memorable passage he claimed that the previous industrial peace, the passing of which so many deplored was but a sham, 'the peace of slavery ... the stillness of death' and he concluded with the claim that 'the awakening had been a long time coming but it had come at last'.[9] Despite its enthusiastic reception, the mere fact that this speech had to be made, the very reference to the fact that many people were apparently contrasting current discontents with previous stability, coupled with the *Advertiser's* own comment that Hancock 'had failed to convince' a very large percentage of his own men[10] is perhaps indicative of a further build up of uncertainty amongst the rank and file.

The evidence that the attitude of the Watnall men to the dispute was significantly different and that there was rather less militancy is not entirely conclusive. For example it must be admitted straight away that the main source of information, the local newspaper, seems to devote much less space in its reporting to the progress of the events at Watnall. This does not necessarily mean there was less to report, but merely that the editor felt it was more removed from the centre of interest of the majority of his readers. Nonetheless it does seem that enough evidence exists to draw the conclusion already indicated. Perhaps the most significant was the early intervention

in the dispute of Colonel Lancelot Rolleston, the owner of
Watnall Hall, a friend of T.P. Barber and, with him, a pillar of
the local Conservative constituency association. Very soon
after the strike began, Rolleston publicly announced his intention to mediate between men and management. On three
occasions he turned up apparently uninvited at Watnall
miners' meetings in Kimberley, speaking at some length in
favour of a compromise. What is especially interesting is that
on two of these occasions he was elected to chair the meeting
and his argument that the gap between the two sides was
insufficient to justify the breach was greeted with at least a
measure of enthusiasm. Indeed at one meeting, two interjec-
tions from the floor that the strike was unnecessary went
apparently totally unchallenged.[11] Moreover, when at the
third meeting, he embarked on a fairly crude attempt to
divide the men from their union leaders by arguing that 'the
employees were familiar with the pits and the management
and could judge better than the officials of the association
whether the management were speaking the truth', seems,
oddly enough, to have produced no reaction at all.[12] Finally
when, not surprisingly, Hancock and his colleagues decided
that Rolleston's mediation was rather less than helpful and
therefore rejected it, the *Advertiser* wondered 'whether they
have the support of the mining community'.[13] Of equal
interest too is the reaction at Watnall to Markham's intervention of 1 February.[14] A meeting at Kimberley on the 3
February, two days before the Central Committee was due to
consider the Markham proposals, was apparently so enthusiastic about them that NMA officials were hard put to damp
things down.[15] Certainly as it turned out, the Watnall men
then met again, two days after the Central Committee and
agreed to support the decision,[16] and a meeting a week later
on 15 February was notable for a succession of speeches on the
justice of the cause.[17] However it must be emphasised that
none of the reports of these Watnall meetings convey anything of the fire and excitement which seem to have been a
characteristic of the Eastwood gatherings, especially that
addressed by Hancock on 18 February (see above). Finally, it

may well be significant that, while inevitably as the strike dragged on and the suffering increased, there was at Eastwood never any public articulation of the obvious fact that, sooner or later, they might well be driven back to accept the owner's terms, at Kimberley this was very much the case. At a mass meeting on 20 February, the chairman while emphasising their determination to win and arguing that he was not wavering, yet went on to wonder seriously how much longer they could hold out.[18]

In the end however, the divisions which opened up in the men's ranks were not so much between Watnall and the Eastwood pits as within the hitherto apparently united body of the Eastwood men themselves. As late as 25 February, the feeling at Eastwood had apparently been as firm as ever. This much can be concluded from a meeting called to consider yet another unfortunate attempt at intervention by Arthur Markham. His first suggestion was that the MFGB should intervene but this came to nothing when he found it impossible to contact the Federation's president Enoch Edwards.[19] Whereupon he suggested that the dispute might go to a conference under the aegis of the National Conciliation Board set up by the Conciliation Act of 1896. This evoked considerable and loudly applauded criticism from two speakers at the meeting, John Goddard and Reuben Reeve, and the latter not only used the word 'interfered' to describe Markham's action but also went on to speculate how this might affect the MP's further prospects in the constituency.[20] However, as it turned out, this was in effect the last manifestation of united defiance, and resistance seemed to crumble away. Almost out of the blue, formal negotiations were opened between the management and employees and a conference met on Wednesday 26 February in which an augmented Central Committee of sixteen representatives, led by Hancock, faced the employers team of Fryar, T.P. Barber, Robert Barber the company's lawyer, and three of the individual colliery managers. The meeting adjourned until after 6 March after a lengthy session, which apparently produced optimism on all sides, and at the second meeting after a further adjournment, agreement was reached on a package to be put to the men.[21]

It is not entirely clear whence the initiative came which ended the deadlock. The *Advertiser* certainly believed that it came from the employers: 'Mr Fryar', it reported, 'has shown a very generous spirit and a desire to end the conflict'.[22] What seems a likely explanation is that by now, both sides were feeling pretty desperate. Given his earlier gloom about the continuing economic viability of the Eastwood pits, Fryar cannot have been at all pleased at the extensive loss of profits the company had sustained. Equally the men could hardly be happy with the outcome for it gave them precious little: on the issue of the price list, face-workers gained virtually nothing and banksmen and main-road workers secured marginal increases. On the issue of non-union labour, Hancock was forced to accept a form of words which fell rather short of the closed shop principle he had been seeking. Finally it was a matter of no small moment that the NMA had paid out no less than £20,000 strike pay in the duration of the dispute. While the men's acceptance of these terms may perhaps be regarded as an indication of their desperate state, nonetheless there was considerable resentment generated which surfaced when the agreement was put to them and fresh divisions opened up. At Watnall, not surprisingly, but also at Brinsley and Underwood, the terms were accepted not only practically unanimously, but even with a degree of enthusiasm. At Moorgreen the acceptance was more grudging and assurances were demanded which, presumably, the officials were able to give. However, at High Park, there was real trouble. Here considerable dissatisfaction was expressed with the price list together with the articulation of a demand to use shovels for coal loading rather than screens which sifted out the smaller coal and could quite clearly affect a coal getter's weekly earnings. However this issue of screens versus forks was almost certainly a 'try-on' by the men, for owners generally in the industry had made it clear that there was no room for negotiation in this matter. The unpleasantness boiled up into an outright rejection of the advice of both Hancock and the Central Committee representatives and the High Park men decided to stay out. This was a hopeless struggle but it went on for more than a month before the men reluctantly accepted the agreement and returned to work at the end of April.[23] That the High Park men felt that they had been betrayed by their colleagues in the other pits was indicated by a letter to the *Advertiser*, which claimed that it had been originally agreed that the strike should only end when everyone agreed to go back.[24]

The persistence of such feelings of resentment in the mining community as a whole after the strike was settled is a matter of some uncertainty. Whitelock, as usual, takes an optimistic line, claiming that 'the workmen settled down quickly'.[25] Moreover, he believed that the problems at High Park were dispelled once the men realised the benefits of Fryar's mechanisation policy in terms of easier and therefore more profitable coal getting.[26] There is indeed some evidence for this. A measure of militant feeling — or lack of it — is provided by the low turn-out at an NMA demonstration at Eastwood on 18 July, when Mrs Bruce Glasier and the Scots miners leader Bob Smillie were to speak on the theme of 'Labour and Socialism'.[27] Moreover, perhaps even more significant was the apparent relative ease with which the Eight Hours Act was applied in the Barber Walker pits. In Eastwood no real problem seems to have arisen: Hancock came to address the local miners on the implication of the Act only to discover that a negotiating group from the Central Committee had already come to terms with Fryar on the hours and meal breaks issues. There was moreover an arrangement to review the situation if any grievances arose and on this basis meetings at Eastwood and Kimberley confirmed the agreement.[28]

Yet, under all this surface of sweetness and light, there was more than a residue of discontent. Speaking at Beauvale in the Autumn of 1908 Arthur Markham referred to reports of 'considerable dissatisfaction' arising from Barber Walker's failure to honour 'the full spirit and the intention of the agreement'.[29] That this was not simply Markham indulging his proclivity for dangerous meddling was illustrated by the revival of the dispute over prices paid for machine cutting in January 1910. Nor is it surprising, in view of previous events, to discover that the centre of the disturbance was High Park.

In effect, the cause of the trouble was not so much the introduction of machine cutting rather than an attempt by the men to maintain existing wage levels. There is no doubt that Fryar was under a lot of pressure: he was worried by the generally declining productivity of the Eastwood pits and especially by the effects of the recession.[30] Nonetheless his reaction was rather brusque. In the first place he singled out High Park as being a special problem and warned that if the trends in profitability continued, then it might well have to close. The only solution he could see was to cut both wages and labour force, the latter by as much as 20%. When taxed with the problem of what was to happen to those who would be out of a job, Fryar merely replied that they would be employed 'as opportunity presented itself'. The seriousness of the situation was reflected by the rapid arrival on the scene of a team of NMA officials led by the newly elected president, W.H. Carter, but they were unable to make any headway, whereupon the High Park men totally rejected Fryar's offer.[31] Nor was it long before the trouble spread to adjoining pits, namely Brinsley and the deep hard seams of Moorgreen. An attempt was made to defuse the situation by the employers' appeal to the Midland Counties Coal Association but although this body's recommendation was, hardly surprisingly, acceptable to Barber Walker, it cut no ice with the men.[32] However it was a slow burning situation rather than a sudden explosion and it was in fact not until the beginning of June when the firm finally took decisive action by issuing termination of employment notices to some 1,500 of its employees at the three collieries.[33] In a very real sense, what we have here is a dispute over new technology and its likely effect on conditions of work and the very existence of jobs. Equally, as the dispute developed, it is noticeable that divisions immediatley opened up once more in the men's ranks. Thus there is precious little evidence of any real solidarity and especially the idea of standing together in the face of a common threat. In this situation, the company's role, as expressed by Fryar, was simply to play for time, not only on the grounds of the slightness of the men's financial resources, already run down by the earlier conflict, but also the undeniable fact that its losses were rather less when the pits were idle than when they were working.[34] Moreover, Fryar was well aware of the dissensions within his opponents' ranks and sought to capitalise on them very early on with his suggestion for a ballot, originally made in a letter to NMA President Carter.[35]

The men's reactions can be gauged by reference to expressions of opinion by the union (the NMA), the Eastwood Central Committee and the individual pits (the last as expressed at pit-head and other mass meetings). In fact the Central Committee played only a marginal part in the dispute and largely seems to have taken the view that the owners' offers were not unreasonable. At the outset it declared itself in favour of arbitration and when this proved abortive, it even went so far as to endorse Fryar's suggestion for a ballot, although with the proviso that it should be extended to all the pits and not simply those in dispute. In a sense, the NMA proved even more equivocal. Initially it strongly backed the men's rejection of the employers' association's mediatory terms and Carter continued to make prominent appearances at meetings at all the pits and not just those affected by the dispute. But, as the dispute came towards the end of its first month, the official union line began to soften quite perceptibly, the reason being simply the financial situation. Thus, Carter himself drew attention to this at an Eastwood meeting in the middle of July,[36] and with lock-out pay costing in excess of £500 per week on top of the estimated £30,000 the 1908 dispute had cost the union, the underlying nature of his concern was clear enough. Equally, the NMA was acutely conscious of its continued failure to settle a strike resulting from similar causes which broke out at Clifton colliery in September 1909.[37] A further measure of its growing anxiety was the union's decision, taken at the end of June, while the dispute was scarcely more than a fortnight old, to refer the matter to the MFGB, but not even the central body could find a way out of the impasse.[38]

The company's lock-out notices terminated on the 15 June and immediately not only does disunity among the men become even more apparent, but also a fair measure of confusion. Right at the outset, there was a clear reversal by High Park, whose earlier hard line attitude had contributed significantly to the conflict, but now suddenly for no discernible reason declared itself in favour of arbitration.[39] Both Brinsley and Moorgreen (hard seams) reaffirmed their positions and at a meeting of men from the former, it was roundly asserted that there simply was no basis for arbitration since 'the machines were an utter failure and there was no chance of getting near the level of eight shillings per day'.[40] Moreover, the men in dispute received a measure of support from their colleagues at Moorgreen (soft seams), Underwood and Watnall and there was even some suggestion at a Watnall meeting of approaching the High Park men to persuade them to see the error of their ways on the issue of arbitration.[41] Possibly as a result of this pressure, High Park not merely came back into line but now went one better by instructing James Alton, their representative on the NMA council, to request that 'the county ... be balloted to come out in order to settle this ... dispute'.[42]

As the dispute dragged on, inevitably the tension began to rise between those locked out and those still working. By the time the dispute had entered August, although the NMA was now desperately looking for a way out by way of arbitration[43] it still felt it necessary to give its leave to the three pits still in operation to hold a strike ballot if this were deemed necessary.[44] By the end of that month, a good deal of resentment was being expressed by the men who were out, coupled with calls for a ballot of the remaining 1,500 men, on the issue of a strike.[45] And it was indeed this issue which opened up another rift. Apparently by mid-September the discontent expressed was such that even the Central Committee felt constrained to make its first real intervention by agreeing to hold a ballot.[46] The decision caused an immense furore. While Underwood and Moorgreen (soft) agreed, the Watnall men led by their representatives W. Brown and W. Lilley refused point blank to take part, whereupon the Committee, apparently fearful of making the division obvious, reversed its decision.[47]

Following this flurry of excitement the conflict dragged on
into the Autumn of 1910 in a singularly desultory fashion with
no one apparently willing or able to break the deadlock. As
early as the second week in August, the local newspaper had
roundly castigated 'the apathy and indifference ... [of both] ...
the masters and the men' which it called 'positively astound-
ing' in view of the serious actual and potential damage being
done to the community.[48] But neither this nor the economic
and financial pressures seem to have had much effect on
men's decisions until, late in November, the indefatigable
Arthur Markham managed to break the deadlock. Markham,
undeterred by his experiences in 1908, had early expressed a
concern[49] and, as the year wore on and a second general
election over the House of Lord's dispute became ever more
imminent, was anxious to clear the decks of any complicating
issues. To cut a long story short, he summoned both the
Central Committee and Fryar to meet him in London and, as
a result, a meeting of 24 November agreed on a return to work
on the 1 December after some 26 weeks.[50]

The conclusion of this, the second long drawn out industrial struggle within eighteen months, was remarkably similar
to the first in the sense that the men had achieved virtually
nothing for all their efforts. The settlement of November 1910
was not a settlement at all: rather it was an agreement to give
Fryar's original proposals a six month trial run, although
some safeguards were written in to ensure that contractors'
wages were at least eight shillings per day. Nor was the
atmosphere of ill-feeling really assuaged. While the company's view was that the matter worked out well,[51] local opinion
was far less sanguine. After only two months of the trial
period, the *Advertiser* commented: 'Judging by the opinion
which is freely expressed by the mining community, the new
arrangements ... are not working as satisfactorily as the men
could wish'.[52] Whereas hitherto the centre of militancy seems
to have been High Park, now it switched to Brinsley. The
Brinsley men had been particularly annoyed by the hasty way
in which the dispute had been concluded and it was noticeable
that, while their mass meeting had accepted the terms, 'a good

deal of dissentient feeling was displayed and ... many re-
frained from voting at all'.[53] There were further mutterings
towards the end of May when the company, apparently
without reference to the union, introduced new prices paid
for 'filling'.[54] Moreover, when the six month period ended
and it became apparent that there were still unresolved
grievances at the three pits, Brinsley took a noticeably harder
line than the other two. Moorgreen and High Park were
apparently persuaded by the intervention of the Central
Committee and the NMA President to accept that the terms
were reasonable and they were not likely to lose money as a
result, but the Brinsley men would not back down and
demanded that the question be taken to arbitration.[55] And so
the last vestiges of the dispute dragged on as the panel of
arbitrators (three NMA nominees and three coal-owners)
found themselves unable to agree and the whole sorry business was subsumed in the national coal strike of 1912.[56] Finally
it is perhaps worth reiterating that, as in 1908, Watnall had
made itself conspicuous by its failure to stand with the other
pits and thus aborted the Central Committee's initiative of
September 1910, perhaps the one occasion during the conflict
when a co-ordinated response looked a possibility.

What now seems sufficiently clear is that the confusion, ill-
feeling and sheer exhaustion (both mental and financial)
resulting from four years of near-continual industrial unrest
made it unlikely that the men were in any position to act
effectively when they were involved in the national Minimum
Wage Strike which commenced on 1 March 1912.

At both Eastwood and Kimberley, considerable unease
had been expressed about the prospects of a conflict in the
early days of the year. The chairman of a miners' meeting at
Kimberley on 8 January expressed very serious doubts as to
the wisdom of the course of action and this was echoed by a
letter to the press which deplored the 'unreality' of the miners'
claim and accused the NMA officials (especially Hancock and
Bunfield) of going out of their way to stir up strikes.[57] This was
perhaps a little hard, but some credence was given to it by
Hancock's emphasis on the need to take this opportunity to
bring Leen and Erewash wage rates into line (8 January) and

his call three days later for no surrender on the issue.[58] Moreover, as the notices were handed in by the men, the *Advertiser* claimed that there was 'no militant spirit at Eastwood and the men have no real grievances'.[59] And in this of course, as we have already seen, they did not differ from the majority of their colleagues in the rest of the Nottinghamshire coalfield.

Certainly, relationships between men and employers did not seem to be unduly disturbed. Although the Butterley Company took the opportunity to close permanently the small, loss-making Plumptre pit at nearby Langley Mill, Fryar took no such provocative action. On the contrary, he won for himself some praise from the local press by his action to see that all concessionary coal had been delivered before the strike began[60] and then by his willingness to help out families suffering real hardship.[61] Equally the men had wanted to carry on working at the company's request for an extra day before the strike actually began as a means of ensuring a rapid return ultimately, but this had been vetoed by NMA officials.[62]

Basically the men's attitude was one of resigned support for the strike with an increasing concentration on very necessary relief work as the distress began to mount quite perceptibly by the end of March. Although the Central Committee took the lead here, there does in fact appear to have been a very real and perhaps remarkable closing of the ranks within the community as a whole. Not only was there co-operation from the Churches and the employers (in the person of Fryar) but also from the local urban district council which had hitherto kept itself very much aloof from such matters. But in spite of this co-operation, the distress was such that cases were coming in faster than could be dealt with and a report at the end of March claimed that while the committee had dealt with 150 cases in the previous week, yet another 150 had come to light.[63] The effect of this on the morale of men who were already doubtful about the point of the whole exercise can well be imagined. The run up to the second national ballot was marked both by the feeling that there was no real alternative but a return to work[64] and with a bitterness against the leadership: 'You can take it from me', an unnamed union branch official said, 'that the men are disgusted with the whole business and with their leaders'.[65] Moreover, perhaps equally indicative were the results of the ballot in the Eastwood area. It would appear that many miners simply did not bother to vote — thus the turnout at Watnall was less than 50%[66] — and at Moorgreen and Underwood, not only was the voting number low, but there was reported to be a large number in favour of a return to work.[67] If Nottinghamshire in general seems then to have been one of the less militant areas in the English coalfields, then it would appear that the Eastwood pits were even less enthusiastic for the struggle than was the county as a whole.

The conclusion of the 1912 strike action thus brought to an end a remarkable period in the industrial history of Eastwood in the years immediately before 1914. For almost five years there had been unrest. As an inevitable result the community had been subjected to tremendous strain, especially on the men's side.

Two related questions needed to be asked in the light of these developments: to what extent was the Eastwood case typical of the Nottinghamshire coalfield and what explanation can be offered for the failure of the miners to maintain effective solidary action? In both instances, it is as well to remind ourselves of the major issues at stake: wage rates, the introduction of mechanised coal cutting and the principle of the closed shop. As we have seen in Part II these were matters of continuing concern throughout the coalfield as a whole in this period. Not only were they a cause of general dissatisfaction and unrest but they resulted in open conflicts of similar length, and presumably similar bitterness, in communities other than Eastwood.[68] Equally, the response of the NMA was largely in character, for while Hancock and his senior colleagues maintained a high profile and, initially at any rate, 'talked tough', the union's essential moderation and desire to bring about an accommodation with the owners was frequently apparent.

On the reasons for the failure to maintain solidarity, it is helpful to recall the contradictory theoretical frameworks, drawn from the works of Thompson and Gilbert, outlined in Part I. It will be remembered that the former saw successful working class action being based on the formation of institutions like trade unions and friendly societies which would both provide social support and raise political consciousness. As we have noted above, the Eastwood miners had the support of the county association but in addition took pains to create their own local institutions, for co-ordinating their action, notably the Central Committee and the Relief Committee. While the latter did much useful, indeed necessary work, the former was ultimately less than successful as initial enthusiasm gave way to disillusion and division. By 1912, and with the onset of the Minimum Wage agitation, it was becoming increasingly clear to Eastwood men, as well as miners across the county as a whole, that prolonging the conflict was unlikely to bring them much by way of material advantage. Nor equally is there much evidence that Thompson's belief in a developing political consciousness was being realised, in spite of the indefatigable efforts of Willie Hopkin to promote a radical, even socialist programme. One of the dangers of this line of argument is that there is a tendency to identify too readily assertive industrial action with a commitment to Socialism. The development of the NMA in these years with its continued commitment to Lib-Labism has already been noted. On balance there does not seem to be any evidence to suggest that Eastwood members were any different to the generality of the county association's membership.

Indeed, increasingly as the evidence is considered it becomes abundantly plain that Eastwood was in no sense the typical mining village, socially homogeneous, closed and set apart, which provided the first alternative model in Gilbert's typology.[69] Rather, it was an amalgam of his second and third models: mixed in occupational composition, influenced by the pull of an expanding greater Nottingham and subject to powerful influences exerted by the coal-owners. Moreover in Eastwood, as indeed elsewhere in the coalfield as a whole there needs to be remembered the existence of the butties, forming a significant stratum within the mining community which in a very real sense was set apart from the generality of the miners and with interests which necessarily diverged. Moreover, with the emergence of Joe Birkin, this group now had an able and energetic leader and his influence was already being felt even at this early stage in his career. If we accept the force of Gilbert's analysis, it soon becomes apparent as to why Eastwood behaved as it did rather than, for example in the manner of the 'red' villages he examines in the South Wales coalfield. Further reinforcement of the argument may also be provided by comparing Eastwood with Hucknall which Gilbert also subjected to detailed scrutiny in support of his general thesis.[70] Certainly there are some interesting points of similarity as well as significant differences but the conclusion above all which seems to come across most strongly is that the nature and effectiveness of collective action in a working class community is extraordinarily dependent on individual cir-cumstances in each separate instance. Moreover, it is plain that only 'where there was a clear sense of collective identity' was such action likely.[71] This then may well be the most plausible explanation for the outcome of events in Eastwood before 1914.

As for the owners themselves, perhaps the most surprising result was that the bruising experience of the five years did not destroy their faith in the concept of a commonality of interest between them and their employees. Fryar in particular in the latter stages was concerned to be conciliatory, and the policy of looking after general welfare was not only to be continued but to be much extended when the company moved into the Dukeries coalfield in the inter-war years.[72] Both employers and miners had reacted in the way they had as a result of economic pressures in large part outside their control: the fluctuations in the market for their product; the inevitable exhaustion of the coal reserves within the pits; the impact of new technology; the demand for a 'minimum' wage level. The acuteness of the conflict over these issues is made especially clear by their detailed examination in a relatively small mining community but, it can be argued that there are impor-tant longer term conclusions to be drawn from the localised experience of Eastwood in these years of conflict.

References

1. *Kimberley and Eastwood Advertiser*, 10 and 24 January 1908. Thus at one meeting in the third week of January it was reported that one speaker was 'frequently interrupted by the call 'Are we downhearted', the responding cheers being loud and long'.

2. *Advertiser*, 7 February 1908.

3. *Ibid*.

4. *Ibid*.

5. *Ibid*.

6. *Advertiser*,14 February 1908.

7.   *Ibid*.

8. *Advertiser*, 21 February 1908.

9. *Ibid*.

10. *Ibid*.

11. *Advertiser*, 3 and 10 January 1908.

12. *Advertiser*, 17 January 1908.

13. *Advertiser*, 21 January 1908.

14. See above.

15. *Advertiser*, 7 February 1908.

16. *Advertiser*, 14 February 1908.

17. *Advertiser*, 21 February 1908.

18. *Advertiser*, 28 February 1908.

19. One is inclined to speculate whether Edwards was making himself deliberately unavailable.

20.   Reeve was one of Moorgreen colliery's representatives on the Central Committee. *Advertiser,* 28 February 1908.

21.   *Advertiser,* 28 February; 6 and 13 March 1908.

22.   *Advertiser,* 28 February 1908.

23.   G.C.H. Whitelock, *250 Years in Coal: The History of Barber Walker and Company Ltd* (published privately nd) p. 45.

24.   *Advertiser,* 20 March 1908.

25.   Whitelock, *250 Years in Coal,* p. 45.

26.   *Ibid.* p. 47.

27.   *Advertiser,* 24 July 1908.

28.   *Advertiser,* 25 June 1909.

29.   *Advertiser,* 20 November 1908.

30.   Whitelock, *250 Years in Coal,* p. 47; *Advertiser,* 17 June 1910. The impact of the recession was such that pit-head prices of coal fell by something like 13% between 1908 and 1910: for figures see A.R. Griffin, *Mining in the East Midlands 1550-1947* (Frank Cass, 1971), table on p 208.

31.   *Advertiser,* 7 January 1910.

32.   Whitelock, *250 Years in Coal,* pp. 47-8.

33.   Whitelock, *250 Years in Coal,* p. 48; *Advertiser,* 3 June 1910.

34.   Whitelock, *250 Years in Coal,* p. 48.

35.   *Advertiser,* 17 June 1910.

36.   *Advertiser,* 15 July 1910.

37.   A.R. Griffin, *The Miners of Nottinghamshire, Vol. I* (Department of Adult Education, University of Nottingham, 1955), p. 198.

38.   *Advertiser,* 1 July 1910.

39. *Advertiser*, 17 June 1910.

40. *Advertiser*, 24 June 1910. This was a riposte to a claim made earlier by Fryar that the effectiveness of the machines was such that *average* daily rates would be well up to former levels (*Advertiser*, 17 June).

41. *Advertiser*, 24 June 1910.

42. *Ibid*.

43. Early in the month the union formally referred the dispute to the National Conciliation Board and by the end of August it had apparently become so desperate as to make two abortive approaches to the Midland Coal Owners Association. See *Advertiser*, 5 August, 26 August, 2 September 1910.

44. *Advertiser*, 5 August 1910.

45. *Advertiser*, 2 September 1910.

46. *Advertiser*, 16 September 1910.

47. *Advertiser*, 23 and 30 September 1910.

48. *Advertiser*, 12 August 1910.

49. *Advertiser*, 1 July 1910.

50. See: *Advertiser*, 18 and 23 November, 2 December 1910. Whitelock, *250 Years in Coal*, p. 48; Griffin, *Miners, Vol. I*, pp. 158 and 198.

51. Whitelock, *250 Years in Coal*, p. 48; and 'Proc. of Joint District Board, 1912' (reproduced in A.R. Griffin, *Miners, Vol. I*, p. 198).

52. *Advertiser*, 3 February 1911.

53. *Advertiser*, 2 December 1910.

54. *Advertiser*, 26 May 1911.

55. *Advertiser*, 23 and 30 June, 28 July 1911.

56. *Advertiser*, 13 October 1911.

57. *Advertiser*, 12 January 1912.

58. *Advertiser*, 12 January 1912.

59. *Advertiser*, 16 February 1912.

60. *Advertiser*, 1 March 1912.

61. *Advertiser*, 15 March 1912.

62. *Advertiser*, 1 March 1912.

63. *Advertiser*, 29 March 1912.

64. *Advertiser*, 29 March and 5 April 1912.

65. *Advertiser*, 5 April 1912.

66. *Advertiser*, 5 April 1912.

67. *Advertiser*, 5 April 1912.

68. Although the work carried out by Griffin, to which extensive reference has been made in Part II, gives us a good overall picture, it would seem desirable for further research to be undertaken on the extent of unrest in communities across the coalfield. This might best be achieved by reference both to local newspapers and the *Annual Reports of the Board of Trade on Strikes and Lock-outs*.

69. See above: page 6.

70. D. Gilbert, *Class Community and Collective Action: Social Change in Two British Coalfields 1850-1926* (Oxford, 1992) pp. 206-244

71. *Ibid.*, p. 255.

72. See above: Part III.

VI

Aftermath and Conclusion

Today the casual visitor to the Erewash Valley would probably find it difficult to envisage the events described above.
The decline and virtual disappearance of the British coal-
mining industry is here indeed an accomplished fact. The last
working mine closed after the 1984-5 strike and the transfor-
mation of the physical geography is largely complete. In no
way now would Eastwood be taken for a colliery town and
some of the outlying villages, like Greasley and Moorgreen,
with their well maintained houses and trim, neat gardens are
positively reminiscent of the 'stock broker' belt of the Home
Counties. Vestiges of the past are still there in the community.
For example, old miners do not just disappear overnight
although they will gradually fade away over a period of time.
The Barber family is still in possession of Lamb Close . The
house itself, once at the centre of a web of collieries, now
nestles peacefully in the gently rolling Midlands countryside.
As a commentary on the extent and pace of change, this
essentially rural scene could hardly be more graphic or
evocative.

It would certainly be taking things too far to claim that the
events of 1907-12 were a truly pivotal sequence which determined the history of the following eighty years. On the other
hand, it would be true to say that they were important insofar
as they encapsulated important trends from the past and
influenced future developments. At its heart this was a crisis
about the nature of industrialisation and about how a particular industry should be organised and the assumptions and

values on which industrial relations should be based. The differing, developing responses to this situation have been sketched out in Section I and, in this analysis, the firm of Barber Walker — both the proprietorial family and successive general managers — fits easily into the tradition of the paternalistic employer, operating on the assumption of a commonality of economic interest with the workforce and exercising a considerable degree of social control over it. As the company's apologist, Whitelock, made perfectly clear, it took a considerable pride both in technological innovations and in the provision of extensive welfare facilities — housing, spiritual, educational and leisure — for its employees. And, if it can be said that this was pursued on a pragmatic, even hit-or-miss, basis in Eastwood, at Harworth in the newly developing Dukeries coalfield post 1920 a more planned approach was possible. Although R. J. Waller's study of this does not make quite so much detailed reference to Barber Walker, it is quite clear that the development of the model village at Bircotes was very similar to what was being done by other companies at villages like Ollerton, Bilsthorpe and Blidworth. Here then was the opportunity provided by a complete *tabula rasa*, to create a community from scratch and so much under the employer's control that there was talk of 'a new industrial feudalism'.[1] Moreover, the company now managed finally, both in Eastwood and at Harworth, to rationalise its equivocal attitude to trade union activity by coming to an agreement with George Spencer's new industrial union the NMU.[2] And yet, in spite of all the careful planning, the outcome was hardly the success for which the company had hoped. The outbreak of the six months Harworth dispute in September 1936 in effect marks the failure of the paternalist approach, thus in a sense confirming what had been foreshadowed in 1907-12.[3] In any case the issue was to be overtaken by more general events, namely the Second World War and the return of a Labour government committed to public ownership of the mining industry.

On the other side of the debate the conclusion is even more bleak for the employees, especially for those who believed in the efficacy of working-class solidarity. As Section I has indicated there was always the conflict of traditions within the working-class response to industrialisation: the one counselling acceptance and deference to the employer, thus mirroring the latter's paternalistic aspirations; the other emphasising the importance of consciousness and prepared to undertake action which might ultimately (perhaps inevitably) prove confrontational. In Eastwood in this period this dichotomy is quite clear and equally clear is the uncertainty and confusion it engendered among the miners in the crisis of 1907-12. Nor was this all for, as was made clear in Section III, the counter tradition of deference had thrown up a new, influential leader in the person of Joseph Birkin. Birkin came to prominence too late to have much direct influence on the events of 1907-12 but thereafter he came to assume the dominant role in subsequent events. Above all the company saw in him the man with whom it could do business in the concern to secure effective control of the workforce.[4] Alan Griffin, undoubtedly the major authority, is quite clear that 'this likeable demagogue exercised considerable influence over his members' and moreover, as a result, the NMA branch at Moorgreen colliery 'assumed the shape of a company union'. But Birkin was destined to exercise his influence on a far wider stage and was to play a major part in the inception of the breakaway industrial union after the 1926 strike. Again, Griffin's judgement is starkly unequivocal: 'If any one man can claim to be the father of the Spencer union it is ... Birkin rather than Spencer himself'.[5]

Inevitably the comparison between 1926 and 1984-5 was always bound to be made, first by those on the ground and then by academics.[6] Equally, it may be seen as straining credibility to attempt to draw a direct line between the conflicts in the Nottinghamshire coalfield across seventy years. Yet in all honesty, the issues at stake are the same: the appropriateness or otherwise of responses by workers in their trade unions to changing economic conditions. One especially bleak conclusion to be drawn from 1907-12 and indeed from the later disputes of 1926 and 1984-5 is that solidarity disintegrates under the pressure of rapid change.

But if the recent, brutal, contraction of the coal industry is anything to go by, then the alternative ideology of co-operation, as advanced by the latter-day breakaway union, the UDM, is hardly encouraging for men desperately anxious for the future of themselves, their families and their communities. For much of the last 100 years, the story of coal and coal-miners has been one of instability and decline, with all that means for an industry which, by its very nature, finds it hard, even near-to impossible, to adapt to changing conditions.

Yet, in spite of everything, the idea of solidarity may well have achieved an ultimate triumph, albeit limited, and in an unexpected form although, regrettably, not in Nottinghamshire. As what was left of the industry was moved back into private ownership, in the case of Tower Colliery, hard by 'Red' Mardy, the one deep mine left in Wales, there emerged the possibility of a buy-out by the workforce, using initially their redundancy money. On 1 January 1995 this became a reality with a take-over ceremony the irony of which, with the singing of the International and the Red Flag, was duly noted by the media.[7] Thus the tradition of solidarity seems to have found a new form in some sort of odd harmony with late twentieth-century notions of popular capitalism. Although no more perhaps than a footnote in the history of a once great and extensive industry, the venture's success or otherwise may be of more than passing interest to future historians.

References

1.   R. J. Waller, *The Dukeries Transformed: The Social and Political Development of a Twentieth Century Coalfield* (Oxford, 1983) *p.75*, quoting a report from the *New Statesman*, 24 December 1927.

2.   See A.R. Griffin, *The Miners of Nottinghamshire, Vol. II, 1914-1944* (Allen and Unwin, 1962) and C. P. Griffin: *Nottinghamshire Miners Between the Wars: The Spencer Union Revisited* (Department of Adult Education, University of Nottingham, 1984) for the details of this episode.

3.   For details, again see A.R. Griffin, *Miners, Vol. II* and C. P. Griffin, *Nottinghamshire Miners*.

4.   See G.C.H. Whitelock's account, *250 Years in Coal: The History of Barber Walker and Company Ltd* (published privately nd), chapters XVII and XVIII. In fact Whitelock becomes positively eulogistic about Birkin's qualities, especially his skill as an orator.

5.   A.R. Griffin, *Miners, Vol. II*, especially pages 97, 116-7, 171 *et seq*, 220, 276.

6.   See C.P. Griffin, *Nottinghamshire Miners*, especially the Introduction and Section V. For the 1984-5 conflict in general, see W.J. Morgan and K. Coates, *The Nottinghamshire Coalfield and the British Miners' Strike* (Department of Adult Education, University of Nottingham, 1989).

7.   See especially the report in *The Guardian* 3 January 1995.